CULTURES OF THE WORLD

Serbia and Montenegro

Cavendish
Square
New York

Published in 2021 by Cavendish Square Publishing, LLC
243 5th Avenue, Suite 136, New York, NY 10016

Copyright © 2021 by Cavendish Square Publishing, LLC

Third Edition

Library of Congress Cataloging-in-Publication Data

Names: King, David C., author. | Nevins, Debbie, author.
Title: Serbia and Montenegro / David C. King, Debbie Nevins.
Description: Third edition. | New York : Cavendish Square Publishing, 2021. | Series: Cultures of the world | Includes bibliographical references and index. | Audience: Ages 10 (provided by Cavendish Square Publishing) | Audience: Grades 4-6 (provided by Cavendish Square Publishing)
Identifiers: LCCN 2019059507 (print) | LCCN 2019059508 (ebook) | ISBN 9781502655912 (library binding) | ISBN 9781502655929 (ebook)
Subjects: LCSH: National characteristics, Serbian--Juvenile literature. | National characteristics, Montenegrin--Juvenile literature. | Serbia and Montenegro--Juvenile literature.
Classification: LCC DR1940 (ebook) | LCC DR1940 .K56 2021 (print) | DDC 949.71—dc23

Editor, third edition: Debbie Nevins
Designer, third edition: Jessica Nevins

Find us on

CONTENTS

SERBIA AND MONTENEGRO TODAY

SERBIA AND MONTENEGRO ARE TWO SEPARATE COUNTRIES, BUT that wasn't always the case. They are located in the Balkan region of Southeast Europe, on what is sometimes called the Balkan Peninsula. This landmass is located to the east of Italy and extends eastward to the Black Sea. Montenegro, the smaller of the two countries, borders the Adriatic Sea, its coastline tucked between those of Croatia and Albania. Serbia, which borders Montenegro to the northeast, is a landlocked country in the middle of the Balkan landmass.

The Balkan region is a place where "East meets West"—where the religions and cultures of Europe collide with those of the former Ottoman Empire, which was centered in present-day Turkey. In the Balkans, Christianity meets Islam, and within Christianity itself, the Roman Catholic Church and Protestant denominations of the West encounter the Orthodox Church of the East. In this part of the world, even alphabets bump up against each other. The Latin alphabet of the West butts up against the Cyrillic alphabet of the East. In Serbia, the Cyrillic alphabet is the official writing system, while in Montenegro, Cyrillic and Latin are considered equal.

Serbia and Montenegro share a great deal of history, culture, ethnicities and language. During much of the 20th century, they were part of Yugoslavia, a federation of states that also included Slovenia, Croatia, Bosnia and Herzegovina, and Macedonia. As that union fell apart in the latter part of the century, several of the countries became embroiled in a decade of war. The Yugoslav wars of the 1990s were a series of separate but related conflicts—a complex mix of ethnic hostilities, wars of independence, and insurgencies.

At the center of the strife was Serbian strongman Slobodan Milosevic. He and his supporters had a nationalist vision of a "Greater Serbia," a centralized Serbian state encompassing the ethnic Serb—populated areas of Croatia, Bosnia and Herzegovina, Montenegro, and all of Kosovo. Some nationalists envisioned an even greater Serbia, including parts of Albania, Bulgaria, Hungary, and Romania. In any event, the imperialist plan fueled a campaign of "ethnic cleansing" and genocide against non-Serbs living in these areas. History has recorded atrocities perpetrated by Serbs against ethnic Albanians and Bosniaks.

For a short few years in the early 21st century, Serbia and Montenegro tried to exist as one united country, but the arrangement didn't work out. Since 2006, they have been independent nations.

The sad history of the 1990s still plagues Serbia today. Yugoslavia is no more, Milosevic is dead, and with Montenegro and Kosovo both having declared independence, Serbia is smaller than ever. The question for Serbia today is: What kind of country does it want to be? In the years following the Milosevic era, the international community was wary of Serbia. Serbs were seen as "the bad guys." Tourists stayed away, and sporting events were canceled. However, Serbia has taken steps to soften its image and align with Europe. Its application to join the European Union (EU), an economic and political union of over two dozen member countries that share common economic, social, environmental, and security policies, speaks to its ambitions for peace and democracy.

Montenegro, too, is attempting to recreate itself as an independent nation. Although the break from Serbia was approved by a small majority of its citizens in a 2006 referendum, there are many ethnic Serbs living in the country who are not happy with this outcome. Also, many Serbs, for their part, consider Montenegro to be an integral part of Serbia.

Much of this feeling can be traced to what is called "the Kosovo Myth," a legendary story that celebrates Serbian and Montenegrin nationalistic glory. Most countries have a sort of origin myth that defines their vision of themselves as a people; it resonates in the patriot heart, creates a sense of identity, and provides justification for historical actions. Often, such stories are based on true historical events that are then mythologized, or engrandized—made larger than life.

This image depicts the legendary Battle of Kosovo.

For these two nations, the accounting of the relatively obscure 1389 Battle of Kosovo—in which Christian Serb armies battled Ottoman (Turkish Muslim) invaders—became, over the centuries, a heroic legend of loss and martyrdom to the Serbian/Montenegrin people.

Kosovo itself—a disputed territory that had been an autonomous province of Serbia, but which declared independence in 2008—is another obstacle for Serbia to overcome. The revered Kosovo battlefield of history and legend is, after all, located there. Today, though, the region is home to a vast majority of ethnic Albanians, not Serbs. Serbia has not officially recognized Kosovo's independence (as of January 2020), but it has begun to normalize relations with the government of Kosovo in accordance with the Brussels Agreement of 2013.

Serbia's virulent nationalism and its component of racism has cooled for the time being, though it appears to lie not far beneath the surface. Occasional incidents at inter-Balkan sports events, for example, speak to these barely suppressed emotions.

Serbia and Montenegro stand at the dawn of a new opportunity. Both countries have much to offer, from magnificent landscapes to natural resources, and from folk arts and fine arts to delectable cuisine. Europe is waiting, with open arms. The world is waiting too.

GEOGRAPHY

A rainbow shines above the mountains of
Durmitor National Park in Montenegro.

SERBIA AND MONTENEGRO ARE TWO different countries that used to be one, but geography stays the same no matter where national boundaries are drawn. Both are countries on the Balkan Peninsula, a region in Southeast Europe that is bounded by the Adriatic Sea to the west, the Ionian Sea to the southwest, the Aegean Sea in the south and southeast, and the Black Sea to the east. The northern border of the Balkan Peninsula is a matter of some controversy, and even the designation of the region as a peninsula is rejected by many geographers. However, Serbia and Montenegro are located in that part of Southeast Europe, no matter what its geographic designation is. In fact, Southeast Europe is now the preferred name for the Balkan region.

Both countries are places of rugged, mountainous beauty. Visitors are awed by the steep canyons carved through imposing mountains,

This map of the Balkan region focuses on Serbia and Montenegro, with Kosovo shown as a country separate from Serbia.

and by the clear, swift streams at the bottom of narrow gorges. In other places, the beauty is more serene, as in the peaceful farm villages.

Without Montenegro, Serbia is a landlocked nation, and without Serbia, Montenegro is a rather small country, smaller than the US state of Connecticut.

A QUICK HISTORY

Serbia and Montenegro were both once part of Yugoslavia, a much larger nation that existed in different forms and under different names throughout much of the 20th century. Throughout most of its existence, it was made up of six constituent republics—Bosnia and Herzegovina, Croatia, Slovenia, Macedonia, Serbia, and Montenegro. It became a communist country in 1945, and in 1963 it took the name the Socialist Federal Republic of Yugoslavia (SFRY). Serbia at that time included two Socialist Autonomous Provinces, Vojvodina (voy-voh-DEEN-ah) and Kosovo.

During the fall of communism in the late 1980s and early 1990s, four of the republics that made up Yugoslavia declared their independence. This triggered a four-year civil war, and by 1996 only two republics remained in Yugoslavia— Serbia and Montenegro—along with the two provinces controlled by Serbia, Kosovo and Vojvodina. Serbia and Montenegro broke apart into two separate countries in 2006. Kosovo declared independence in 2008. Although that status is still in flux, this book treats Kosovo as a separate nation. It is not included in statistics relating to today's Serbia.

SERBIA

The Republic of Serbia is located in the central Balkans in Southeast Europe. Its capital is Belgrade, in the north-central part of the country. Serbia is surrounded by eight countries, including Kosovo, its former autonomous province. To the north and northeast, it borders Hungary and Romania; to the southeast, Bulgaria; and to the south, North Macedonia. On its southwestern border are Kosovo and Montenegro, and to the west, Serbia borders Bosnia and Herzegovina and Croatia.

Serbia covers 29,913 square miles (77,474 square kilometers) and is slightly smaller than the US state of South Carolina. Surrounded on all sides, it has no direct access to the sea. Its terrain is extremely varied, ranging from the rich fertile plains of the north to the craggy, mountainous region of the south.

THE PANNONIAN PLAIN   In the northern region of Serbia, the landscape of the Autonomous Province of Vojvodina is defined by the Pannonian Plain (also known as the Pannonian Basin), a region of grassland similar to the Great Plains of North America. Millions of years ago, the area was covered by the Pannonian Sea. Over time, alluvial deposits from the mountains gradually filled in the sea, leaving rich layers of soil, which make this ideal agricultural land.

The plain extends along the Danube River and its tributaries, including the Sava, Tisa, and Drava. The danger of floods has been reduced by building dikes and canals. More than half of Serbia's farms are located in these fertile lowlands.

Rolling grasslands make up the Pannonian region of Serbia.

The climate here is more extreme than in the other parts of the country. Hot, humid summer days often bring temperatures above 100 degrees Fahrenheit (37.7 degrees Celsius), while the long, cold winter sees temperatures below -10°F (-23.3°C).

THE INTERIOR HIGHLANDS   The central region of Serbia is a hilly land crossed by rivers and other waterways. The great Y-shaped valley of the Morava River system runs south to north, forming the main population center of the country. To the west, the jagged peaks and broad ridges of the Dinaric Alps run northwest to southeast, parallel to the Adriatic coast. To the east, the limestone ranges of the Serbian Carpathian Mountains meet the Balkan Mountains. Farther south, Serbia extends into the Rila-Rhodope mountain system.

The Balkan Mountains extend from Serbia eastward through Bulgaria to the Black Sea.

Since 1975, the United Nations Educational, Scientific and Cultural Organization (UNESCO) has maintained a list of international landmarks or regions considered to be of "outstanding value" to the people of the world. Such sites embody the common natural and cultural heritage of humanity and therefore deserve particular protection. The organization works with the host country to establish plans for managing and conserving their sites. UNESCO also reports on sites that are in imminent or potential danger of destruction and can offer emergency funds to try to save the property.

The organization is continually assessing new sites for inclusion on the World Heritage List. In order to be selected, a site must be of "outstanding universal value" and meet at least one of ten criteria. These required elements include cultural value—that is, artistic, religious, or historical significance—or natural value, including exceptional beauty, unusual natural phenomena, or scientific importance.

As of January 2020, there were 1,121 sites listed, including 869 cultural, 213 natural, and 39 mixed (cultural and natural) properties in 167 nations. Of those, 53 are listed as "in danger."

Montenegro is home to three cultural sites and one natural site. These include the Natural and Culturo-Historical Region of Kotor on the Adriatic Coast, as well as Durmitor National Park in northern Montenegro. In addition, Montenegro shares in two other sites. With Italy and Croatia, it is part of the fortifications listed as the Venetian Works of Defense Between the 16th and 17th Centuries: Stato da Terra–Western Stato da Mar. Also, Montenegro is included along with three neighboring countries in a serial property, a group of 28 sites that make up the Stecci Medieval Tombstone Graveyards, shown above. Montenegro also has six additional tentative sites awaiting UNESCO consideration.

Serbia has four cultural sites on the World Heritage List. These include the ancient Roman fortress Gamzigrad-Romuliana, Palace of Galerius in the east; Stari Ras and Sopocani, a collection of medieval monasteries, churches, and town buildings in the Raska region of southern Serbia; and the medieval Studenica Monastery in central Serbia. In addition, Serbia shares in the Stecci Medieval Tombstone Graveyards.

Serbia has submitted an additional 12 places to UNESCO for World Heritage consideration. They are now on UNESCO's Tentative List.

Serbia's highest peak is Midzor in the western Balkan Mountains. It straddles the border between Serbia and Bulgaria, and is 7,116 feet (2,169 meters) high.

Although parts of the Dinarics and the Balkans display spectacular scenery, large areas can seem bleak and desolate. In winter, cold winds called the *bora* roar down from the north. The winds do not bring much snow, but the cold is bitter and unrelenting.

Generally, the region has a moderate continental climate, but there can be extremes in both summer and winter. January temperatures average 32°F (0°C), for example, but there can be long stretches with the thermometer below 14°F (-10°C). Summer temperatures average 68 to 72°F (20 to 22°C) but can reach 86°F (30°C) for several days.

The highlands are on an unstable section of tectonic plates, making earthquakes a constant danger. A serious earthquake in 2010, centered near the city of Kraljevo in the central part of the country, killed 2 people, injured more than 100, and caused a good deal of structural damage in the region.

MONTENEGRO

Smaller than Serbia, Montenegro covers 5,333 square miles (13,812 sq km), stretching from the Adriatic Sea on its southwest to Serbia on its northeast. Its capital is Podgorica. To its southwest, it touches a small bit of coastal Croatia, and to the west and northwest, it borders Bosnia and Herzegovina. To the east, it shares a border with Kosovo, and on the southeast, its border with Albania stretches to the Adriatic coast.

The name Montenegro is Italian for "black mountain." In Serbo-Croatian, the name is Crna Gora (TSUR-na GORR-uh).

THE COASTAL REGION   Montenegro's coast is a narrow, rocky strip of land that hugs the shoreline of the Adriatic Sea. At sea level on the fjord-like Gulf of Kotor, greenery provides a lush contrast against the gray backdrop of the Dinaric Alps, which rise steeply behind the shore. The white sand beaches of resort towns draw tourists from all parts of Europe. Many of the fishing villages have long histories, like the town of Budva, one of the oldest on the

The Danube River is one of the world's greatest rivers. It is the second-longest in Europe, and it carries and deposits millions of tons of sand, clay, gravel, and other matter each year. It begins in Germany's Black Forest and flows through or borders another nine countries: Austria, Slovakia, Hungary, Croatia, Serbia, Romania, Bulgaria, Moldova, and Ukraine.

About 10 percent of the Danube flows through Serbia, where it is called the Dunav. It passes through the capital, Belgrade, where it meets the Sava River. The Sava is one of several major tributaries that flow into the Danube in Serbia. Others include the Tisa, Tamis, Mlava, Karas, Nera, and Pek Rivers. From Belgrade, the Danube flows southeast to form a 142-mile (228.5 km) portion of Serbia's northeastern border with Romania. At this point, the Danube separates the southern Carpathian Mountains from the northwestern foothills of the Balkan Mountains. The Serbian side of the river here is part of Djerdap National Park.

It is on this section of the river that four gorges form the high cliffs of the Iron Gate. The normally placid Danube picks up great speed as it rushes through the gorges, shrinking to its narrowest width (about 500 feet, or 150 m) at the Great Kazan Gorge (shown above). There, the river flows fast and very deep, twisting and turning as it gushes through a narrow gorge with cliffs more than 2,000 feet (610 m) high. Downstream, the huge Iron Gate Dams harness the Danube for two hydroelectric power plants. The two dams, built in 1972 and 1977, also help with navigation through this difficult section of the river.

The Danube is an international waterway and carries many cargo vessels and cruise ships. In 1999, river transport on the Danube became difficult following the bombing of three bridges in Serbia during the Kosovo War. The resulting debris was finally cleared in 2002, and a temporary pontoon bridge, which further hampered river traffic, was removed in 2005.

This aerial shot of the Montenegrin coast shows the town of Budva on the Adriatic Sea. Its historic Old Town is the walled section of red-roofed buildings extending out from the mainland.

Adriatic. Over the centuries, Budva has been home to ancient Phoenicians, Illyrians, Greeks, and Romans, and later Venetians, Austrians, and Serbs. Unlike neighboring Croatia, Montenegro has no large, inhabited islands off its coast.

The coast enjoys a Mediterranean climate of dry, sun-filled summers, with temperatures averaging 75°F (24°C) in July. Winters are rainy and cool. January temperatures average 45°F (7°C) but rarely fall below freezing.

THE KARST REGION   A few miles inland, the land features limestone outcroppings called karst terrain. This is a landscape in which water and carbon dioxide (from the air) form a mild acid that slowly erodes soft areas of limestone. This creates deep holes called chimneys, as well as long depressions and underground caves that carve honeycomb-like webs, often extending over several miles.

Located on the border between Montenegro and Albania, Lake Skadar (also called Lake Scutari or Skadarsko Jezero) is the largest in Southern Europe. The lake is a national park in both countries.

Once an arm of the Adriatic Sea, the lake is now separated from the sea by a narrow strip of land. Steep mountains rise dramatically above the water on the west and northwest. Six rivers flow into Skadar, and a seventh— the Bojana River—flows out the southern end and drains into the Adriatic.

Small picturesque villages dot the shoreline around the lake. Several are well known for their old monasteries and fortresses, some dating back to the 13th century. The ruins of Fort Grmozur, for example, dominate a small island in the lake (shown above). Built by the Turks in 1843, it was one of a line of defense fortresses during the period of Ottoman rule. In 1878, the fortress was captured by Montenegrin troops, and it was used as a prison until an earthquake in 1905 caused part of it to collapse.

The point at which Montenegro, Kosovo, and Albania meet is one of the most imposing mountain regions in the Balkans. The highest mountain in Montenegro is here, Zla Kolata, at 8,314 feet (2,534 m). Located in the Prokletije range, the mountain straddles the border between Montenegro and Albania.

THE DINARIC ALPS   In the northern part of Montenegro, the Dinaric Alps create ruggedly dramatic landscapes. This is the location of Durmitor National Park, a World Heritage site known for its extraordinary beauty. It is home to around 50 peaks higher than 6,500 feet (2,000 m)—including Bobotov Kuk at 8,274 feet (2,522 m)—and numerous glacial lakes. The park is where Zabljak,

The Tara River Canyon extends from Bistrica in Montenegro to Hum in Bosnia and Herzegovina. The Montenegrin section, shown here, is part of a protected site.

the highest town in the Balkans, at 4,777 feet (1,456 m) above sea level, is located, as well as Black Lake, one of the park's most scenic glacial lakes. The park is probably best known for its breathtakingly deep canyons, including the Tara River Canyon, with the deepest gorges in Europe.

RIVERS AND LAKES

In Montenegro, clear, fast-moving rivers flow through steep-sided canyons into the Adriatic Sea. In Serbia, the rivers flow northward and northeastward into the Danube, which flows to the Black Sea. The Danube, one of Europe's great rivers, runs through Serbia for about 225 miles (362 km) and forms part of the border with Romania for another 142 miles (229 km).

There are more than 100 natural lakes in the two republics. Some are in depressions left by the glaciers of the last Ice Age (which receded about 12,000 years ago). People call these glacial lakes the "eyes of the mountains" because of the clear blue of the water. Other lakes fill hollows near the coast of the Adriatic Sea, including the largest in the region—Lake Skadar (Skadarsko Jezero in Serbo-Croatian)—which straddles the Montenegrin border with Albania.

Two people enjoy a peaceful afternoon in a kayak on Lake Skadar.

ANIMALS

This southeastern part of Europe has drawn hunters, hikers, fishers, and naturalists from many countries. The forested mountain slopes support a rich array of large animals, including brown bear, roe deer, wild boar, and the goatlike chamois. These species still thrive in spite of having been hunted for several centuries.

Some species, such as wolf and lynx, have declined largely because of farmers' efforts to get rid of predators with poison. Both species survived by moving deeper into the mountain regions; new environmental laws are also offering protection. Two new species, introduced in the 20th century, are thriving—the raccoon dog, brought from eastern Asia, and the muskrat, from North America.

Game birds have also been plentiful, but populations declined severely in the 1980s and 1990s because of the war and environmental pollution. Common species include quail, pheasant, grouse, and partridge, plus waterfowl such as geese and various species of ducks.

The waterways of Serbia and Montenegro are known for their abundance of fish and birds. The wetlands along the Danube and Sava Rivers have been one of the largest nesting grounds for birds in all of Europe. Different species

The sturgeon in the Danube have been overfished, and dams have cut off their migration routes. Unlike some neighboring countries, Serbia has resisted imposing a complete ban on fishing the species. Some species of sturgeon are already extinct in the Danube.

have made use of different parts of the ecosystem. Cormorants and pelicans are found in the deeper waters, for example, while waders such as herons and egrets stand in shallow water to wait for their prey. Meanwhile, shorebirds such as ibis and spoonbills use their unique beaks to dig into the wet sand. The thick reeds form small floating islands in the slow-moving channels, providing excellent nesting sites for a variety of songbirds, such as warblers, rakes, little bitterns, and others.

The variety of birds and abundance of fish have also drawn birds of prey. Osprey, for example, are great fishers, and white-tailed eagles, harrier hawks, and red-footed falcons dine on fish as well as other small creatures.

Both bird and fish populations have declined sharply because of overfishing and pollution. The Danube and the Black Sea, for example, were once primary sources of caviar. Caviar is the processed eggs of large fish, such as sturgeon, but overfishing has nearly destroyed the sturgeon population. Because a sturgeon can live more than 60 years and each female lays more than 2 million eggs, catching just one female sturgeon has a powerful effect on the future sturgeon population.

Other fish, many of them of commercial value, have also declined, including the wels, a huge catfish species that can weigh up to 440 pounds (200 kilograms)! A number of these species are found only in the Danube River and its tributaries. This includes a species of herring that has adapted to freshwater and the Romanian bullhead perch.

PLANTS

The Serbian and Montenegrin regions of the Balkans are ancient lands, with many species of plants dating far back in time. Some species of trees, such as the horse chestnut, originated here an estimated 65 million years ago and then

A boardwalk crosses a wetland area in the Jankove Bare Reserve, part of Kopaonik National Park in Serbia.

spread to other parts of the world. There are more than 5,000 plant species in the countries, and many of them are native to the region. In certain places, the antiquated farm methods used have enabled some areas to support wetlands and meadows that bloom into glorious fields of wildflowers in the spring. More modern farming methods would change most of these areas into cropland.

Forests still cover almost one-third of Serbia and 40 percent of Montenegro, mostly in the mountain regions. In the eastern part of Serbia, deciduous forests cover most of the Carpathian and Balkan Mountains, while mixed deciduous and coniferous (evergreen) forests are found in the lower elevations of the northern Dinaric Alps. In the southern and western Dinarics, most of the forests have been cleared, causing serious erosion.

Along the Adriatic coast, plants accustomed to a Mediterranean climate have adapted well to the long, dry summers. These plants include palm, olive, fig, orange, and lemon trees, as well as pomegranate shrubs.

SETTLEMENT PATTERNS

The geography of the region has influenced where and how people have settled over the centuries. For example, isolated mountain regions have remained thinly settled, with widely scattered villages and a few towns. Farms tend to remain small in the mountains, while farms—and even farmhouses—on the plains are larger. During the time of the Roman Empire (about 250 BCE to 400 CE), some of the coastal areas developed into prosperous city-states. Farther inland, overland trade routes led to some towns becoming important trade centers.

Belgrade, Serbia's capital, offers a good example of how location influences the importance of a community. In ancient times, Belgrade's fortress—Kalemegdan—occupied a strategic position, dominating the confluence of the Danube and Sava Rivers. Many major military powers fought for control of that location, among them Romans, Celts, Huns, Magyars, Byzantines, Slavs, Avars, Bulgars, Turks, and Serbs. Historians say that Belgrade has been destroyed and rebuilt more than 40 times.

This view of Belgrade, as seen from the air, shows the Sava River, which flows into the Danube, seen in the distance.

In the 20th century, especially after World War II (1939—1945), the development of modern industry and transportation has led to dramatic changes in settlement patterns. Large numbers of people have migrated from rural areas to cities and towns. In 2019, around 67 percent of Montenegrins and 56 percent of Serbians were living in urban areas.

Podgorica, shown here in the summertime, is the capital of Montenegro.

INTERNET LINKS

https://www.discover-montenegro.com/geography
Montenegro's karst geography is discussed and pictured on this travel site.

https://www.nytimes.com/2018/08/22/travel/montenegro.html
This travel article about Montenegro includes a map, many photos, and relevant information.

http://serbia.com
This Serbia travel site has a large section dedicated to the country's natural features.

https://whc.unesco.org/en/statesparties/me
https://whc.unesco.org/en/statesparties/rs
UNESCO's pages for Montenegro (/me) and Serbia (/rs) link to the countries' World Heritage properties.

HISTORY

The Tabula Traiana, an ancient Roman carving on the Danube River, speaks to the long history of civilization in Kladovo, Serbia.

THE HISTORY OF HUMANS IN THE Balkans goes back some 200,000 years—earlier than in any other part of Europe. However, a clear picture of how people lived does not emerge until the Neolithic Period (New Stone Age), about 7000 BCE. Between 7000 and 3500 BCE, people were living in settled farm villages in the Pannonian Basin, along the Sava and Danube Rivers. These societies, which archaeologists call Old Europe, created craftwork in pottery and copper and had a primitive form of writing.

After 3500 BCE, seminomadic groups began moving into the Balkans from the steppe region of what became Russia. These early newcomers were well-organized warriors, using horse-drawn war chariots—the most advanced war technology of the time. They built stone fortresses on the hills and cliffs above the river valleys. By about 1000 BCE, the strongest of these groups, known as Illyrians, built a powerful kingdom, which survived until a series of conquests by the Romans began in 168 BCE.

2

The Tabula Traiana, dating from around 103 CE, is an ancient Roman plaque, carved along the side of the Danube River, honoring the construction of roads and bridges during the time of Emperor Trajan. It was originally 72 feet (22 m) lower on the cliffside, but the construction of a hydroelectric dam in the late 1960s deepened the river in that spot. The monument was therefore moved above the waterline.

AN AGE OF EMPIRES AND MIGRATIONS

Even before the mighty Romans moved in, the Illyrians had felt the humiliation of conquest at the hands of two famous Greek conquerors—first, Philip II of Macedon, and then his son, Alexander the Great. They controlled the region for a short time in the mid-300s BCE. The Romans needed nearly two centuries to subdue the Illyrians, finally gaining complete control in 9 CE. The Illyrians became important to Rome's efforts to protect the empire from outside invaders. The Illyrians were excellent soldiers, and five of their officers rose to become emperors of Rome.

THE ROMAN EMPIRE

One of the Roman emperors, Diocletian, who was struggling to save the empire from waves of invaders, divided the empire in 285 CE. The division became permanent in 395 CE, with a boundary along the Sava and Danube Rivers. This became a cultural boundary as well as a political one. Rome ruled the lands to the west, and Constantinople—today the Turkish city of Istanbul—ruled lands to the east, known as the Byzantine Empire.

The Romans had a lasting influence on the region. Their genius for engineering and building is still evident in the remains of Roman arenas, roads, aqueducts, and bridges.

For more than a thousand years, great migrations into Europe from Asia altered the course of history in this region. Waves of people, representing different cultures and ethnic backgrounds, pushed west and southwest from Central Asia. The Romans called these people "barbarians," a Greek word meaning "outsiders" or "strangers."

One such group, called the Goths, began moving into the Balkans around 200 CE, slowly forcing the outnumbered Romans to withdraw. Over a period of 200 or 300 years, other groups followed the Goths: Huns, Bulgars, Visigoths, Avars, and others.

By the late 400s, these invasions had greatly contributed to the total collapse of the Western Roman Empire. The invaders pillaged and burned as they conquered. They did not respect the advanced culture of Rome, so they thought nothing of destroying beautiful buildings, sculptures, books, or other works of art. With the fall of Rome, Europe entered a transition period. Gradually, new societies emerged, forming kingdoms that were the forerunners of modern nations, including France, England, and Spain. Italy and Germany remained divided into dozens of small kingdoms and principalities until the late 19th century. The Balkans remained splintered even longer.

THE EMERGENCE OF SERBIA

In the 6th century, another group of tribes, the Slavic people, migrated into the Balkans from the north. Like the other groups, the Slavs lived by farming and herding. They soon gained enough control of the western Balkans to call the area Sclavinia—the Land of the Slavs.

During the Middle Ages, from roughly the 700s to 1300, the Slavs found their lands fought over by several empires: the Franks, Magyars, Bulgars, and the armies of the Byzantine Empire. These empires rose and fell, conquered and withdrew.

Adding to the chaos of the Middle Ages was the failure of any Slavic group to gain control over more than a small area. Practically all of the societies in the region that became Yugoslavia were Slavic, but they were divided into a number of warring tribal groups. Isolated by the mountains and separated by different tribal histories, people felt their strongest loyalty to their village and their large, extended families. Occasionally, a strong headman, or *zupan* (ZOO-pahn), would unite several villages and gain power over an area large enough to be considered a kingdom. Slovenia, Croatia, Dalmatia, Bosnia, Herzegovina, and Serbia each experienced a brief golden age as a separate kingdom, before being overwhelmed by more powerful empires.

The most important legacy of these short-lived kingdoms was a spirit of nationalism. Centuries later, in the 1800s and 1900s, different Slavic groups looked back to those early kingdoms for an almost mythical history to help prove their legitimacy in forming a nation-state with a home territory and a cultural identity.

In the mid-800s, a Serb kingdom emerged under a zupan named Vlastimir. Vlastimir acknowledged the overall authority of the Byzantine Empire, but he was able to develop a fairly independent kingdom. His relationship with the empire encouraged the patriarch of the Eastern Orthodox Church, a branch of Christianity, to send two monks, Cyril and Methodius, to teach the Bible to the Serb people. In the process, the two brothers devised a new alphabet, based on Greek, known as Cyrillic. This is still the alphabet of Serbia and several other countries, including Russia. Croatia and some of the other countries in the Balkans retain the Roman (or Latin) alphabet, as do most countries in Europe and the Americas. The Montenegrin language can be written with either alphabet.

Over several centuries, the Serb kingdom fell to outside conquerors a number of times before emerging again in the early 1300s under King Stefan Dusan. The kingdom flourished for a short time and even dominated much of the Balkan Peninsula. However, a new power was rising in the East—the Ottoman Empire.

THE OTTOMAN EMPIRE

The Ottoman Turks were Muslims. From their base in modern-day Turkey, they rose to power gradually and finally gained control of a vast stretch of territory, including parts of Southern and Eastern Europe, the Middle East, and North Africa. In 1389, they defeated the army of the Serbs at the Battle of Kosovo ("the Field of Blackbirds"). Serbia became a vassal state of the Ottoman Empire, ruled by the Turks until the 19th century.

The Serbs continued to resist Ottoman control. Occasionally, they found allies in their struggle, such as Russia and the Austro-Hungarian Empire. In 1817, these great European powers forced the Turks to recognize Serbia as an autonomous, or self-ruling, principality within the empire, with Belgrade as the capital. Complete independence was recognized in 1878.

Over the decades that followed, the Serbs steadily tried to expand their borders. They were also involved in efforts to create a larger Slavic state to include all Slavic peoples, even those in Poland and Russia. This effort, called Pan-Slavism, was supported by Russia, the largest Slavic state.

In 1912 and 1913, Serbia was involved in two armed conflicts, called the Balkan Wars. The Balkan League (Serbia, Montenegro, Greece, and Bulgaria) conquered Ottoman-held Macedonia and most of Thrace. Austria-Hungary and Germany were uneasy about Serbia's increase in power during the Balkan Wars. When the heir to the Austro-Hungarian throne, Archduke Franz Ferdinand, and his wife were shot and killed by a Serb nationalist, Gavrilo Princip, in Sarajevo, Bosnia, on June 28, 1914, Austria-Hungary and Germany reacted severely. The incident sparked the Great War, or World War I. On July 28, Austria-Hungary declared war on Serbia. Russia then came to the aid of its fellow Slavic nation and declared war on Austria-Hungary. The chain reaction of declarations of war continued until all of Europe and much of the world were engulfed in the most terrifying war the world had yet witnessed.

THE ORIGINAL YUGOSLAVIA

When World War I ended in 1918, the victorious Allied powers, including the United States, redrew the map of Europe. Four empires had collapsed during the war: the German, the Austro-Hungarian, the Russian, and the Ottoman. Following the idea of self-determination developed by US president Woodrow Wilson, the Allies tried to establish new nation-states that would satisfy the dreams of many ethnic groups who longed for their own national identity.

One result of these efforts was the creation of the Kingdom of Serbs, Croats, and Slovenes, with Peter I of Serbia as king. When Peter's son, Alexander I, came to the throne in 1929, he changed the name of the kingdom to Yugoslavia—the Land of the South Slavs. He also began rule as a dictator, saying it was in the hope of creating greater national unity, but unity was impossible with so many ethnic groups in one region. In 1934, King Alexander I was murdered by Croatian terrorists. The king's cousin Paul then became regent for the 11-year-old heir, Peter II. This meant he would rule until Peter II was old enough to do so himself.

For 500 years, the Ottoman Turks ruled over a mighty empire. For much of that time, the Islamic world represented the world's most advanced civilization. Kingdoms in Europe gained great advantages from Muslim achievements in science, medicine, astronomy, and other fields. Explorers such as Christopher Columbus would not have been able to sail the world's oceans so freely without the technology and techniques they learned from the Muslims.

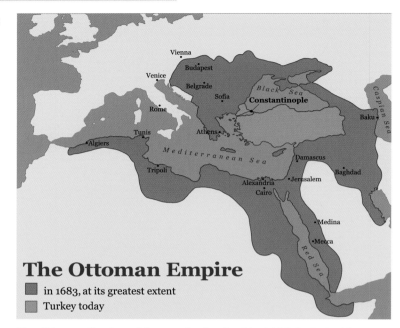

The Ottoman Empire

■ in 1683, at its greatest extent
■ Turkey today

The Ottoman Empire, at its greatest extent in 1683, included Serbia, whose capital Belgrade is noted on this map.

In the 1700s, the Ottoman Empire entered a long period of decline. Internal weaknesses, combined with the advances in weaponry of European countries, began turning the Ottomans into a second-rate military power. In addition, people like the Greeks and Slavs began demanding an end to years of Turkish rule. First, Serbia demanded independence in the early 1800s, followed by Greece in the 1820s. Several times during the 19th century, the great powers of Europe held conferences to decide what to do about the empire they now called "the Sick Man of Europe," sometimes forcing the Ottoman Empire to recognize the independence of one of its provinces.

The end of the empire finally came during World War I. The Turkish leaders sided with the Central Powers, led by Germany and Austria-Hungary. When the Allied Powers, including England, France, and the United States, won, the Ottoman Empire collapsed, and its former provinces either became independent or were made protectorates to be governed by Britain or France.

WORLD WAR II AND MARSHAL TITO

World War II was devastating for Yugoslavia. The conflict caused widespread destruction and cost the lives of one in every ten Yugoslavs. During that same war, a remarkable individual rose to power in Yugoslavia and went on to create, by the force of his rule, a unified state that lasted more than 35 years. His name was Josip Broz, better known as Marshal Tito. Tito rose through the ranks of the Communist Party of Yugoslavia (CPY) in the 1930s and then became the leader of the country's heroic wartime resistance against Nazi Germany.

Early in the war, the Yugoslav government caved in to pressure from Nazi dictator Adolf Hitler and agreed to join the Axis Powers (Germany, Italy, and Japan). However, the Yugoslav army rebelled, overthrew the regent Paul, and placed young Peter II on the throne. Hitler responded by sending an army into Yugoslavia, and when Peter's government fled to England, Hitler divided the country into sections to be ruled by Germany, Italy, and Bulgaria. At the same time, a Croatian pro-Nazi force, the Ustasa, launched a ruthless campaign of rounding up thousands of Serbs and Jews for execution or for deportation to German concentration camps.

The Germans did not count on the fierce resistance put up by two groups of Yugoslav freedom fighters—the Chetniks, led by Draza Mihailovic, and the Partisans, under Marshal Tito. Even though the two groups fought each other as well as the Germans, the Yugoslav resistance prevented Hitler from gaining complete control of the country. By the end of 1944, with aid from the United States and Great Britain, the resistance fighters had forced the Germans to withdraw. Even during the fighting, Tito had set up local revolutionary councils, and these quickly seized control as the Germans left.

THE SECOND YUGOSLAVIA

In November 1945, Yugoslavia became the Federal People's Republic of Yugoslavia, with Tito as prime minister. It was a federation made up of Bosnia and Herzegovina, Croatia, Macedonia, Montenegro, Serbia, and Slovenia. A few months later, the Chetniks lost the civil war, and Mihailovic was executed by the Tito government. In 1963, the country was renamed the Socialist Federal

Josip Broz (1892–1980)—commonly known as Tito—was one of the great military and political leaders of the 20th century. The first half of his life was characterized by struggle and defeat. As a communist, he was regarded as a dangerous revolutionary and was imprisoned several times in the 1920s and early 1930s.

This statue of Tito stands at his tomb, called the House of Flowers, in Belgrade.

During World War II, when he organized the Partisan resistance against Nazi Germany, his heroic stature rapidly emerged. No other country occupied by Germany put up such a spirited resistance as that led by Marshal Tito. Hitler refused to believe that the Partisans could not be defeated, and he committed one army division after another to the task, including a surprise parachute attack that nearly caught Tito. He had to fight his way out of traps several times and was wounded twice. Still, by 1943, his force numbered 250,000.

After driving the Germans from the country, Tito forged a strong sense of national unity and, during the Cold War, managed to follow a policy of "nonalignment" with both the Soviet-led East and the US-led West. Nevertheless, Tito welcomed Nikita Khrushchev, secretary general of the Communist Party of the Soviet Union, and Soviet prime minister Nikolai Bulganin to Belgrade in 1955. He also traveled the world to strengthen Yugoslavia's ties with other nonaligned nations, including India and China.

Republic of Yugoslavia (SFRY), and Tito declared himself "President for Life." Indeed, he ruled the nation as a dictator until his death in old age in 1980.

Tito ruled with an iron hand, maintaining peace among the different ethnic and religious groups. While trying to create a communist nation, with state control of industry and agriculture, he managed to resist the efforts of the Soviet Union to control all the communist countries of Eastern Europe. Although political opposition was not allowed in Tito's Yugoslavia, the people enjoyed greater freedoms than in the more Soviet-dominated countries.

Yugoslavia experienced dramatic growth under Tito, but the 1979 worldwide oil crisis led to major economic woes for the country.

THE CIVIL WAR

After Tito's death in May 1980, the Communist Party regime slowly crumbled. In January 1990, the Communist Party gave up control, and multiparty elections were held. It soon became clear that all the old ethnic, nationalistic, and religious rivalries had only been stifled for all those years, not eliminated. In June 1991, Croatia and Slovenia each declared their independence. This immediately led to fighting between Croatians and the ethnic Serbs' military.

When the ethnic Serbs in Croatia appealed for help, the Yugoslav army, largely controlled by Serbia and Serb president Slobodan Milosevic, joined the fighting, plunging Yugoslavia into a long and bloody civil war. The conflict expanded a few months later when Bosnia and Herzegovina also declared independence. Here, too, a Serb minority took up arms against the majority government, which was controlled by Bosnian Muslims, or Bosniaks, and Serbia again sent Yugoslav army divisions to their aid. In January 1992, Macedonia withdrew from Yugoslavia in a peaceful separation. The two remaining republics in the war-torn country, Serbia and Montenegro, declared themselves to be the Federal Republic of Yugoslavia (FRY) in April 1992.

The civil war engulfed civilian populations when Milosevic orchestrated a Serb policy of ethnic cleansing. The Serbs, who were members of the Eastern Orthodox Church, were determined to rid the country of Bosniaks and Roman Catholic Croatians. In the vicious campaign, thousands of men, women, and children were rounded up. Many were executed and buried in shallow mass graves.

In 1995, Serbia was involved in an infamous massacre in the small town of Srebrenica, Bosnia. More than 8,000 Bosniaks, mainly boys and men, were murdered, and around 25,000 to 30,000 Bosniak women, children, and elderly were forced to leave. The massacre, perpetrated by an army of Bosnian Serbs and a paramilitary unit from Serbia, was eventually deemed to be an act of genocide. More than 10 years later, the International Court of Justice (ICJ) cleared Serbia of direct responsibility for, or complicity in, the massacre. However, it

The Serbian politician Slobodan Milosevic (1941–2006) rose to power in Yugoslavia following the death of Tito. He served as the president of Serbia from 1989 to 1997, and as president of the Federal Republic of Yugoslavia from 1997 to 2000.

He was born and grew up in Pozarevac, a city in eastern Serbia. When Slobodan was a child, his father left the family; some years later, he killed himself. Around the same time, an uncle did the same. Ten years later, Slobodan's mother took her own life as well. The young Milosevic had few friends. His wife, Mirjana Markovic (1942–2019), herself an activist communist politician, had tremendous influence over him throughout his career and was widely rumored to be the "power behind the throne." For that, she was sometimes referred to as "the Red Witch" or the "Lady Macbeth of Belgrade."

Early in his political career, Milosevic became concerned about what he considered the abuse of power in Serbia's autonomous provinces. He thought the ethnic Serb minority in Kosovo, where ethnic Albanians were the majority, suffered a disadvantage in a land that rightfully belonged to them. He advocated for reduced autonomy for the provinces and a strong crackdown on Kosovar separatists. His Serbian nationalism and populist style appealed to many followers in Serbia but also stoked resentment in the other Yugoslav republics.

Milosevic's desire for a "Greater Serbia" for Serbs drove him to war against his neighbors—Slovenia, Croatia, Bosnia, and the Albanians of Kosovo—at various stages in the breakup of Yugoslavia. His ruthless and virulent nationalism led to years of bloodshed, took hundreds of thousands of lives, and earned him the epithet the "Butcher of the Balkans."

On March 11, 2006, while imprisoned in The Hague, Netherlands, Milosevic was found dead in his cell. Since 2002, he had been standing trial before the International Criminal Court for war crimes—representing himself—and the trial was thought to be nearing its end. Since he died before it was over, a judgment was never issued; he was therefore never found guilty of the charges brought against him.

was found responsible for not doing enough to prevent the genocide and not prosecuting those responsible.

THE INTERNATIONAL COMMUNITY INTERVENES

News of these horrors leaked out. The United Nations (UN), reflecting outraged global opinion, first imposed economic sanctions on Serbia and then approved the use of troops and warplanes by the North Atlantic Treaty Organization (NATO) to stop the fighting. The UN also established a War Crimes Tribunal in the Netherlands to investigate charges of "crimes against humanity."

NATO forces managed to stop the fighting, and the Serbs agreed to peace in negotiations held in Dayton, Ohio, at the invitation of US president Bill Clinton. The Dayton Accords were then signed in Paris, France, in December 1995. However, Serbia and Montenegro's troubles were far from over.

WAR IN KOSOVO

Kosovo was one of two autonomous provinces within the Republic of Serbia. Throughout the 1990s, the people of Kosovo called for greater independence. About 90 percent of the people were Albanians, and they wanted their government to reflect that.

Instead of granting greater independence, Milosevic ordered the Serbian army into the province in 1999, where it met stiff resistance from the Kosovo Liberation Army (KLA). Frustrated world leaders again searched for a way to restore peace and end the ruthless ambitions of Milosevic. The UN imposed sanctions again. When that failed, NATO warplanes (American and British) launched bombing raids against Serb positions and industries. The 78 straight days of bombing caused heavy damage and forced Milosevic to withdraw his troops.

By this time, well over 1 million Kosovar Albanians had become refugees, fleeing across the borders into neighboring countries. A UN peacekeeping force moved in, and one of the first steps it took was to oversee elections in 2000.

The entire decade of the 1990s had been consumed by ethnic bitterness and the driving ambition of Milosevic. People were eager for a new beginning,

The North Atlantic Treaty Organization, or NATO, is a mutual defense alliance of member countries from North America and Europe. As of 2020, there are 29 member nations. Formed in 1949 in opposition to communism and the Soviet Union, it has since expanded to include several formerly communist nations, including (as of 2020) several countries of the former Yugoslavia: Croatia, Montenegro, and Slovenia.

Any discussion of Serbia today is complicated by the status of Kosovo. This partially recognized nation is, or was, an autonomous province of Serbia. Since declaring itself independent in 2008, Kosovo has seen a mixed response from the international community. Some nations recognize its independence, and some—notably Serbia itself—do not. It didn't help Serbia that all neighboring nations—Albania, Bulgaria, Croatia, Hungary, Montenegro, and North Macedonia—recognized Kosovo's independence.

Serbia asked the UN's International Court of Justice (ICJ) for an advisory opinion on whether Kosovo's unilateral declaration of independence was in accordance with international law. In 2010, the ICJ stated that international law did not prohibit declarations of independence.

Working through intermediaries, Serbia then began negotiating with its breakaway province. In 2012, the

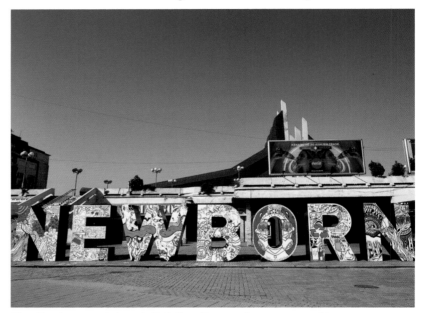

The *Newborn* sculpture in Pristina, Kosovo, is a monument to independence. It was unveiled on February 17, 2008, the day the former Serbian province declared independence.

European Union (EU) began mediating talks aimed at normalizing relations between the two. It was a complex and difficult process, riddled with setbacks, violence, and even murders.

In 2015, Kosovo and Serbia signed a series of agreements in key areas, a major step toward normalizing ties. Kosovo declared it a de facto recognition of independence, but Serbia dismissed that idea. Nevertheless, the measure allowed Serbia to move forward with its negotiations to join the EU by 2025.

and hopes were high for the elections of September 2000. Milosevic lost the presidential election to Vojislav Kostunica. When Milosevic refused to accept the election results, hundreds of thousands took to the streets in massive public protests. Milosevic finally stepped down in early October, and Kostunica was sworn in.

In April 2001, Milosevic surrendered to Serbian authorities. Charged with abuse of power and corruption, he was extradited to the jurisdiction of the International War Crimes Tribunal in The Hague, Netherlands, to stand trial for war crimes and genocide during the civil war.

AN END AND A BEGINNING

The end of Milosevic essentially marked the end of Yugoslavia—but not before more violence sent shock waves through the country. In 2001, Zoran Djindjic became the prime minister of Serbia. Djindjic was pro-Western, pro-democracy, and had long opposed Milosevic. It was he who extradited Milosevic to the International War Crimes Tribunal to stand trial in The Hague. Djindjic was determined to clean up organized crime and corruption in Serbia, and to that end, he created a special tribunal with a witness protection program. There was also no love lost between Djindjic and Kostunica, the Yugoslav federal president at the time.

In March 2003, one month after the Yugoslav parliament approved a constitutional charter that dissolved Yugoslavia and replaced it with the Union of Serbia and Montenegro, Djindjic was assassinated in Belgrade. The murder was found to be masterminded by two leaders of Serbia's most powerful organized crime organization. Both were paramilitary police officers with strong ties to Milosevic. In 2007, a Serbian court found 12 men guilty of the crime, and all were sentenced to prison. Djindjic was shot by a sniper's bullet as he was on his way to meet with Anna Lindh, Sweden's minister of foreign affairs. She herself would be murdered a few months later, stabbed to death in a Stockholm department store by a Serbian assassin.

Nevertheless, Serbia and Montenegro became one country. The union didn't last long. Years of turmoil had left the economy in ruins. Thousands of refugees were homeless, and a residue of bitterness remained among the

The European Union (EU) is a political and economic organization of 27 European member nations as of early 2020.

Supporters of
Montenegrin
independence
celebrate in
Podgorica on
May 21, 2006,
after a referendum
indicated the
majority was in
favor of breaking
away from Serbia.

different ethnic groups. Violence continued in 2004 with some of the worst clashes between Serbs and ethnic Albanians in Kosovo. Again, NATO troops were mobilized.

Montenegro declared independence in 2006, and its separation from Serbia was without major incident. In 2008, after Montenegro recognized Kosovo's independence, Serbia expelled the Montenegrin ambassador to express its anger. However, that blew over quickly, and in general, relations between the former partners are cordial. Each maintains an embassy in the other's capital.

Both countries wish to become members of the EU and are actively pursuing that goal. Both countries have to achieve certain objectives in order to be accepted. For example, in 2013, the European Parliament said Montenegro was on track to achieve EU membership, but it needed to do more to protect media freedom, women's rights, and gender equality. As of 2020, both countries are still working toward acceptance.

Meanwhile, Montenegro joined NATO in 2017, becoming the 29th member of the alliance. The move angered Russia, Montenegro's longtime ally, which views NATO as a direct threat.

INTERNET LINKS

https://www.bbc.com/news/world-europe-17670524
https://www.bbc.com/news/world-europe-17913357
These are BBC News timelines of key events in the histories of Montenegro (top link) and Serbia (bottom).

https://www.britannica.com/biography/Josip-Broz-Tito
The online *Encyclopedia Britannica* provides an article about the life and accomplishments of Marshal Tito.

https://www.lonelyplanet.com/montenegro/background/history/a/nar/ae566540-2a0d-49f0-80bf-2f190e0a9079/360151
Lonely Planet provides a good overview of Montenegrin history.

https://www.nytimes.com/2006/03/12/world/europe/slobodan-milosevic-64-former-yugoslav-leader-accused-of-war.html
The *New York Times* obituary for Slobodan Milosevic provides an in-depth look at his life and legacy.

https://www.nytimes.com/2007/05/24/world/europe/24serbia.html
This article reports on the people who were found guilty of assassinating Zoran Djindjic.

http://www.serbia.com/about-serbia/serbia-history
This Serbian travel site offers a Serbian take on its own history.

GOVERNMENT

The red flag of Montenegro (*top*) is diagonally folded over the red, blue, and white flag of Serbia. Both flags incorporate a double-headed eagle motif.

3

BOTH MONTENEGRO AND THE Republic of Serbia are parliamentary republics. This is a form of democracy in which the executive branch of the government derives its legitimacy from and is accountable to the legislature (lawmaking body), or parliament. The members of the parliament are typically elected by the citizens. In such a political system, the executive branch is made up of a president and a prime minister.

The president is the head of state and is usually a ceremonial figurehead. This person represents the nation on the international stage and is often elected by the citizens, but rarely has much power. The real power—most of the time—resides in the prime minister, the head of the government. This person is chosen, or elected, by the members of the parliament. As in most democracies, the government is defined by and based on a national constitution.

Serbia and Montenegro, having grown out of the communist system of Yugoslavia, are new to this form of government. It hasn't been easy for either country to make this transition. Their short-lived attempt as the Union of Serbia and Montenegro made neither side happy, especially not the smaller, less powerful Montenegro. In 2006, Montenegro declared independence, which by default left Serbia as its own independent nation as well.

In both Serbia and Montenegro, the voting age is set at 18. In Serbia, however, there is the added stipulation that people who are employed may vote at age 16.

SERBIA: THE CONSTITUTION

In 2006, the newly created Republic of Serbia had to draw up a new constitution. The proposed text of the constitution was approved by the National Assembly on September 30 of that year and put to a referendum the following month. After 53 percent of the electorate supported the proposed constitution, it was officially adopted on November 8, 2006. As of January 2020, there have been no amendments.

The constitution declares Serbia to be a nation based on "the rule of law and social justice, principles of civil democracy, human and minority rights and freedoms, and commitment to European principles and values." It establishes that the law is based on "inalienable human rights," that men and women are equal under the law, and that national minorities have special protection "for the purpose of exercising full equality and preserving their identity."

The constitution further declares that Serbia is a secular state, with a separation of church and state. It assigns the Serbian language and the Serbian Cyrillic alphabet as the official language and alphabet. Democratic political rights are guaranteed as political parties are protected, providing they don't advocate forced overthrow of the government or encourage religious, racial, or national hatred. Freedom of information is more broadly granted than in the previous constitution.

As part of the process of economic decentralization—the transition from a centralized, planned economy to a more liberal, free-market economy—the constitution recognizes only private, corporate, and public property. Previous "social assets" no longer exist.

On a social level, marriage is defined as the "union between a man and a woman," meaning same-sex marriage is therefore considered unconstitutional.

In the matter of Kosovo, the constitution addresses the subject right in the very first sentence of the preamble. Kosovo, it states, "is an integral part of the territory of Serbia" with "the status of a substantial autonomy within the sovereign state of Serbia." In other words, the Serbian constitution declares Kosovo to be a part of Serbia, albeit one with significant autonomy (much like Serbia's Autonomous Province of Vojvodina). Kosovo, for its part, disagrees with that assessment and declared its independence in 2008.

SERBIA: GOVERNMENT STRUCTURE

The head of state is the president. He or she is directly elected by an absolute majority of the popular vote (in two rounds if needed) for a five-year term, and is eligible for a second term. The next election at this writing is to be held in 2022. The head of government is the prime minister. He or she is elected by the legislature.

The legislature is the unicameral (one-house), 250-seat National Assembly (Narodna Skupstina). Its members are directly elected from a party list, with a proportional-representation vote in a single nationwide constituency. Under this system, voters around the country choose which political party they support, and seats in the National Assembly are then divided between the parties based on what percentage of the vote each party received nationwide. Members serve four-year terms. As of May 2019, Serbia's National Assembly was composed of 157 men and 93 women; therefore, the percentage of women in the legislature was 37.2 percent.

The judiciary includes a 36-judge Supreme Court, a 15-judge Constitutional Court, and the usual subordinate local courts.

In 2017, Aleksander Vucic became the fifth president of Serbia. He has served in the Serbian government in various roles since 1998, when he was the minister of information for Slobodan Milosevic. In 2012, he became the minister of defense and the first deputy prime minister; then, from 2014 to 2017, Vucic served as the prime minister.

Although Vucic has moved to a more pro-European stance over the years, critics accuse Vucic's government of being authoritarian and autocratic, particularly in terms of its suppression of press freedom. The nongovernmental organization Freedom House, which annually ranks countries according to

President Aleksandar Vucic of Serbia speaks during a press conference after Russian-Serbian talks on December 4, 2019, in Sochi, Russia. Behind him are two Serbian flags.

This building in Belgrade houses the Serbian National Assembly.

how well they uphold human rights, political freedoms, and civil liberties, has issued cautions about Vucic's "de facto accumulation of executive powers that conflict with his constitutional role." In 2019, the organization lowered Serbia's rating from "Free" to "Partly Free" based on "deterioration in the conduct of elections [and] continued attempts by the government and allied media outlets to undermine independent journalists through legal harassment and smear campaigns."

MONTENEGRO: THE CONSTITUTION

The constitution of Montenegro, adopted in 2007, declares the country to be "a civil, democratic, ecological ... state of social justice, based on the rule of law." It guarantees "rights and liberties," prohibits the infliction or encouragement of hatred or intolerance, bans discrimination, and establishes the equality of men and women. It protects freedom of religion and asserts a separation of religion and state. It declares the official language to be Montenegrin, with the Cyrillic and Latin alphabets being equal. However, it allows for the Serbian, Bosnian, Albanian, and Croatian languages to also be in official use.

The constitution further protects individual freedom of thought, expression, association, and assembly. Among other rights, it lists the right to health care. Like the Serbian constitution, the Montenegrin document defines marriage as being between a man and a woman, thereby blocking the legalization of same-sex marriage.

MONTENEGRO: GOVERNMENT STRUCTURE

Montenegro has a president and a prime minister. As in Serbia, the president is directly elected by an absolute majority of the popular vote (in two rounds

A man casts his ballot in a voting station located in a bank in Niksic, Montenegro, in the 2018 presidential election.

if needed) for a five-year term, and is eligible for a second term. The most recent election was held in 2018, and the next is to take place in 2023. The prime minister is nominated by the president and approved by the Assembly.

The legislature is the unicameral Assembly (Skupstina). It is made up of 81 seats, and members are directly elected in a single nationwide constituency by proportional-representation vote, as in Serbia. Members serve four-year terms. In 2019, the Assembly was composed of 62 men and 19 women—featuring 23.5 percent representation by women.

The judicial system consists of a Supreme Court with 15 judges plus a president and deputy president, and a Constitutional Court with 7 judges plus a president, as well as various lower courts.

In 2018, Milo Dukanovic became the country's president; however, he has served as either president or prime minister of Montenegro almost continuously since 1991. Critics describe him as authoritarian and autocratic, and they allege that he has ties to organized crime in Montenegro. In

Milo Dukanovic, then prime minister of Montenegro (*left*), meets Donald Tusk, president of the European Council, in Brussels, Belgium, in 2015.

2010, he was listed by a British newspaper as being one of the 20 richest world leaders. Freedom House sees Dukanovic's control of the ruling party (Democratic Party of Socialists, or DPS) and the government as being a red flag threatening Montenegro's democracy. The organization ranked Montenegro as "Partly Free," citing widespread corruption and cronyism, intimidation of the news media, the "vast personalized power" of Dukanovic, and a correspondingly weak parliament.

INTERNET LINKS

https://www.constituteproject.org/constitution/Montenegro_2013. pdf?lang=en
https://www.constituteproject.org/constitution/Serbia_2006. pdf?lang=en
The constitutions of Montenegro and Serbia are posted in English.

https://freedomhouse.org/report/freedom-world/2019/montenegro
https://freedomhouse.org/report/freedom-world/2019/serbia
Freedom House rates each country's score on upholding citizens' political rights and civil liberties.

http://www.gov.me/en/homepage
This is the official site of the government of Montenegro.

https://www.srbija.gov.rs
This is the official site of the government of the Republic of Serbia.

ECONOMY

Though still joined with Serbia at the time, Montenegro adopted the euro as its currency in 2002, in anticipation of joining the European Union. Some EU financial ministers considered this move premature and "incompatible," but not illegal.

4

JUST AS MONTENEGRO AND SERBIA had to reorganize their governments following the dissolution of Yugoslavia, they also had to redesign their economies. The transitions from centralized communist governments to democracies mirror the transformations from planned to free-market economies.

After the end of communism in Eastern Europe in 1989 and 1990, corresponding with the collapse of the Soviet Union, both countries were well positioned to make these changes. However the war years of the 1990s, under the leadership of Slobodan Milosevic, dealt a devastating blow to both that set them back many years. For Serbia and Montenegro, the greatest war damage was the result of the NATO bombing raids in 1999. The bombing caused nearly $30 billion worth of damage to oil refineries and factories, along with additional billions of dollars of damage to roads, railroads, and power stations. The economic sanctions imposed on Serbia by the United Nations added to the economic disaster. In the year 2000, slightly more than half the labor force was out of work, and inflation continued to skyrocket. Economists correctly predicted that it would take at least 15 years to restore the country to the prosperity levels of 1989.

Once all sanctions were removed in 2001 when the Milosevic regime ended, the economy began to show signs of improvement. However, complex political issues, slow development of private enterprise, and a stagnant European economy at first hindered progress.

Montenegro uses the euro as its domestic currency, though it is not yet a member of the European Union. In 2012, Montenegro began negotiations to join the EU. Serbia, too, officially applied to join in 2009. In order to begin negotiations, Serbia had to first normalize its relations with Kosovo. Montenegro had to take steps to fight corruption and organized crime. Both countries are expected to be admitted by 2025.

WHAT IS GDP?

Gross domestic product (GDP) is a measure of a country's total production. The number reflects the total value of goods and services produced over one year. Economists use it to determine whether a country's economy is growing or contracting. Growth is good, while a falling GDP means trouble. Dividing the GDP by the number of people in the country determines the GDP per capita (per person). This number provides an indication of a country's average standard of living—the higher the better.

In 2017, the GDP per capita in Serbia was approximately $15,100. That figure is considered to be in the medium range, and it ranked Serbia at 111th out of 229 countries listed by the CIA World Factbook. *That same year, Montenegro's GDP per capita was a slightly higher $17,800, ranking 99th, which placed it more or less in the same category as Serbia. For comparison, the United States that year was number 19, with a GDP per capita of $59,500. Other former Yugoslav countries did a bit better—Croatia with $24,700, at number 81, and Slovenia with $34,500, at number 58, had healthier economies. Both Croatia and Slovenia are members of the European Union.*

STATE VERSUS PRIVATE BUSINESS

When Marshal Tito brought the Communist Party into power in 1945, he started the process of having the government take control of Yugoslavia's economy. This was in keeping with the theories of Karl Marx, one of the founders of communism, who wrote that the first step in creating the ideal of communism was to achieve "state ownership of the means of production." State control was achieved quickly, sometimes using force when farm families balked at the idea of collective ownership.

However, going back to private ownership of industry and agriculture has taken longer, and the average person's standard of living remains relatively low compared to European standards. In Serbia, the power utilities, telecommunications company, natural gas company, and other large enterprises remain state-owned. In Montenegro, around 90 percent of formerly state-owned companies have been privatized, including all of the banking, telecommunications, and oil-distribution businesses.

AGRICULTURE

Agriculture has always been an important part of Serbia's and Montenegro's economies. In fact, until the post—World War II years, the great majority of people made a living by farming. Today, however, both countries have become predominantly service economies, with only about 19.4 percent of Serbs and 7.9 percent of Montenegrins working in agriculture. This sector contributes only 9.8 percent of Serbia's GDP and 7.5 percent of Montenegro's.

In Serbia, most farming takes place in the northern regions, particularly in the province of Vojvodina on the fertile Pannonian Plain. Other agricultural regions include the river valleys of the Sava and Danube Rivers. Small farms can also be found scattered throughout the country. In addition, many working families grow grapes for wine or plum trees for the country's favorite plum brandy.

Agricultural parcels of different crops cover the flat Pannonian Plain of Vojvodina in Serbia.

Montenegro's coastline on the Adriatic provides a huge boost to the economy—not, as one might expect, due to the commercial fishing industry, which is quite small, but rather by way of tourism. The 182-mile (293.5 km) stretch of shoreline, with its Mediterranean climate, 120 beaches, seafood restaurants, coves, fjords, and other attractions, lures a growing number of visitors each year.

People enjoy a sunny June day in Old Town, Kotor, in Montenegro.

Tourism brings in three times as many visitors as Montenegro's total population every year and accounts for almost 25 percent of the country's GDP. Numerous luxurious hotels, resorts, yachting facilities, and other hospitality complexes are in various stages of development along the coast, most of them the projects of foreign investors. (The biggest foreign investors in Montenegro in 2017 were Norway, Russia, Italy, Azerbaijan, and Hungary.) In 2017, about 1.9 million international tourists arrived in Montenegro, up 12.9 percent over the previous year. Optimistic forecasts predict an annual growth of 5.5 percent, reaching 3 million tourists by 2027. As the number of tourists rises, so does the number of jobs in the tourism and travel sector.

Montenegro wants to tempt more visitors to explore other areas of the country beyond the coast. It touts its varied landscape of mountainous panoramas; national parks; picturesque lakes, rivers, and canyons; and other outdoor attractions. The country has 10 ski resorts, numerous thermal spas and wellness centers, and various archaeological, historic, religious, and cultural sites to attract tourists and their money.

Farmers mostly grow wheat, maize, sunflowers (for oil), sugar beets, grapes for wine, vegetables—especially tomatoes, peppers, and potatoes—and fruits—primarily raspberries, plums, apples, and sour cherries. Serbia is one of the world's leading producers of raspberries and the 19th-largest producer of wine.

About one-third of Serbian agriculture is devoted to livestock. Dairy cattle, beef cattle, sheep, and pigs are the most important farm animals, along with chickens and geese.

In Montenegro, agriculture plays a smaller role in the economy. Since most of the country is hilly or mountainous, there are few vast, flat areas for large farms. Small family farms that produce crops mainly for their own use are the norm. The country's farmers grow olives and citrus fruits in the coastal regions and other seasonal vegetables and tobacco in the central region. In the north, sheep breeding is common.

Because of its smaller agricultural sector, Montenegro has to import most of its food. Much of it comes from Serbia and other neighboring countries.

Sheep drink from Vrazje Lake in Durmitor National Park in Montenegro.

Workers assemble cars at the Fiat factory in Kragujevac, Serbia.

MANUFACTURING AND MINING

Serbia's main industrial sectors include automotive, mining, nonferrous metals, food-processing, electronics, pharmaceuticals, and clothing manufacturing. Automobile manufacturing is particularly important and includes the production of tires, suspension parts, and electrical system components. FCA Srbija (Fiat Chrysler Automotives Serbia) is a joint venture between the carmaker Fiat and the government of Serbia that operates a plant in Kragujevac. The factory employs about 2,000 employees and produces around 400 cars a day. It manufactures the Fiat 500L, which is sold internationally.

The food and beverage industry is also strong in Serbia. PepsiCo, Nestlé, and Coca-Cola all have factories in the country. Pharmaceuticals and electronics are important too.

Coal mining, as well as the mining of copper, lithium, cobalt, and other minerals, was a major economic sector in Serbia during the Yugoslavia years.

That sector, like so much else, fared poorly during the disastrous Milosevic era, and the mining industry remained stagnant for years. Today, however, Serbia is trying to rejuvenate the business, with the help and funding of international investors. Serbia has around 300 mines being operated by about 20 international companies. Serbia's skilled but relatively low-cost labor force is one attraction that draws investors, as well as its wealth of mineral deposits.

Montenegro also has mining operations, notably aluminum, bauxite, lead, and zinc, but the sector plays a minor role in the country's economy. In fact, manufacturing in general is a shrinking sector.

INTERNET LINKS

https://balkaninsight.com/2018/08/01/montenegro-eyes-record -breaking-tourism-season-08-01-2018
This article provides information about Montenegro's tourism boom.

https://www.cia.gov/library/publications/the-world-factbook/ geos/mj.html
https://www.cia.gov/library/publications/the-world-factbook/ geos/ri.html
The *CIA World Factbook* site provides up-to-date economic statistics, including informative economic overviews for both countries.

ENVIRONMENT

Air pollution causes smog to settle over Valjevo, a city in western Serbia.

5

THE LANDS OF SERBIA AND Montenegro offer spectacular natural beauty—from picturesque farms and fishing villages to wild, snowcapped mountains and deep canyons carved by rushing rivers. Ecologically, however, the picture isn't nearly as pretty. Serbia, in particular, faces overwhelming ecological problems as it struggles to comply with EU standards.

The troubles began with the pollution produced during the years of Communist Party rule, and those problems were compounded by the civil war and NATO bombing.

THE LEGACY OF COMMUNISM AND WAR

When the Communist Party came to power in 1945, it had the goal of transforming agricultural societies into modern industrial and urban nations. While the regime of Marshal Tito achieved considerable success, the cost amounted to an environmental disaster.

Because the Communist Party authorities were so intent on rapid industrialization, they paid no attention to side effects such as air and water pollution. In addition, they used outdated equipment and methods because that was all that was available. Outmoded, coal-burning blast furnaces produced iron and steel, spewing great clouds of black smoke that

A 2019 UN report, "Air Pollution and Human Health: The Case of the Western Balkans," found that the people in this region are exposed to some of the highest concentrations of air pollution in Europe—up to five times higher than acceptable levels. This pollution reduces the average life expectancy in these countries by up to 1.3 years.

hung over the cities. Chemical plants and a new cement industry contributed new combinations of pollutants to the environment. To the planners, the smog-shrouded factory towns seemed to symbolize industrial progress, but the pollutants were poisoning people's lungs, as well as the air, land, and water. The authorities insisted that pollution was only a temporary problem that could be addressed later.

The years of civil war and NATO air strikes in the 1990s also caused widespread damage to the environment. Factories were flattened, mines were flooded, and oil refineries were destroyed, pouring petroleum into rivers and streams. However, large areas of Serbia and Montenegro remain virtually untouched. This is especially true in mountainous regions, where forests and lakes continue to draw tourists and sports enthusiasts from other parts of Europe.

MEASURING THE DAMAGE

In addition to the legacy of communism and war, a public lack of environmental awareness added to the chaos. Farming, for example, contributed to land and water pollution through the heavy use of chemical fertilizers and pesticides to increase production. The waste leached into the groundwater, and from there into streams and lakes.

In those days, making extraordinary changes to the natural world was considered a sign of human might and intelligence. Rivers were diverted, mountains were leveled, wetlands were filled, and Earth's topography was shifted around and contaminated with little thought to anything other than how it would benefit people in the short term.

For example, to increase cropland, the Communist authorities carried out ambitious programs of building irrigation canals and draining wetland areas in the Pannonian Basin. These efforts did increase farmland, but they also had unexpected consequences. They led to increasing salinity (salt content), a common problem with irrigation, and caused erosion and flooding in several areas.

Sewage from urban areas and from cattle and pig farms has further contaminated groundwater with nitrates and phosphates. By the mid-1990s, less than 10 percent of Serbia's wastewater was being treated before it was released into the republic's waterways.

The once-magnificent Danube River suffered enormous damage. Environmentalists point out that this river, one of the longest in Europe, has been like an open sewer flowing through eight countries, serving a population of more than 80 million people. The Danube is, in fact, the most polluted river in Europe. The lake above the Djerdap hydroelectric station in Serbia has been called the "garbage dump of Europe."

Other rivers have also been severely damaged. The Sava River has suffered several oil spills, and the Ibar River had such high levels of phenol that the government shut off the water supply from the Kraljevo treatment plant, one of the largest in the Balkans.

Air pollution has been as serious a problem as the pollution of land and water. The high sulfur content of coal used in antiquated blast furnaces and in home heating units has had a deadly effect on air quality. Motor vehicle emissions have added significantly to the problem. Few controls have been installed on trucks and buses, and enforcement of laws has been lax. Belgrade frequently qualifies as one of the world's most air-polluted cities.

Old plastic bottles and other floating pieces of trash pile up on the shore of the Danube River in Belgrade.

THE IMPACT ON PLANTS AND ANIMALS

Air pollution in the form of acid rain has contributed to the pollution of hundreds of lakes and ponds. These pollutants, including nitrates and phosphates, cause a buildup of algae. The algae growth is more than the ecosystem can handle, leading to a loss of nutrients that kills the algae. Decomposing algae then choke off the oxygen, resulting in the death of fish and other marine life. The dying off of fish in these lakes and ponds has led to an alarming reduction of birdlife throughout the entire region.

The Balkan region, including Serbia and Montenegro, has been known for varied and unusual plant and animal life, but as of the beginning of the 21st century, more than 350 species of plants and animals in the region were listed as endangered. In addition, the years of warfare led many wild animals to seek safety in the mountains of Bulgaria, but now that the guns are silent, many of these animals are finding their way back.

EFFORTS TO PROTECT AND RESTORE

Environmental awareness has developed very slowly in Serbia and Montenegro. In the 1980s, new laws and a constitutional amendment raised the hopes of environmentalists, as did a growing interest in the so-called Green Movement that was sweeping Europe. This awareness was strengthened in the later 1980s, following the news of the world's worst nuclear accident, at Chernobyl in the Soviet Union. As deadly radioactive clouds drifted westward across Europe, people became keenly aware of the fragility of the world's environment and the interconnectedness of its ecosystems.

Since the fighting stopped in the region, the people and the governments of Serbia and Montenegro have shown a new commitment to repairing the damage to the environment and providing better protection in the future. The desire to join the European Union has also provided a strong motivation to clean up the mess to meet stringent European environmental standards. In this, the countries are not alone. Many international aid groups, including UN agencies such as the United Nations Development Programme (UNDP), the World Health Organization (WHO), the Food and Agriculture Organization

(FAO), and the UN Children's Fund (UNICEF), are providing funding, loans, and expertise to help the countries set and achieve environmental goals.

The government of Montenegro declared itself to be "the world's first environmental state," with a pledge to live in harmony with nature. The 2007 Montenegrin constitution itself asserts the right of citizens to a healthy environment. The governments of both Serbia and Montenegro have also signed several international agreements reflecting this new commitment.

INTERNET LINKS

https://balkangreenenergynews.com/tag/serbian-environmental -protection-agency
The Balkan Green Energy News site provides an archive of articles relating to environmental protection in Serbia.

https://www.developmentaid.org/api/frontend/cms/ uploadedImages/2019/06/Air-Quality-and-Human-Health-Report_ Case-of-Western-Balkans_preliminary_results.pdf
This is a downloadable version of the UN environmental report about air pollution in the Western Balkans.

https://www.euronews.com/2018/04/05/serbia-faces-up-to-huge -hazardous-waste-problem-to-meet-eu-environment-standards
This article about hidden hazardous waste sites in Serbia includes a video.

https://www.reuters.com/article/us-serbia-pollution-air/belgrade -joins-worlds-most-polluted-cities-as-farmers-torch-fields -idUSKBN1X3293
This article about air pollution in Belgrade points to the causes contributing to the problem.

SERBS AND MONTENEGRINS

Crowds of pedestrians walk down
a street in Belgrade, Serbia.

6

WHO IS A SERB? WHO IS A Montenegrin? The answers are complicated. The simplest answers are that the citizens of Serbia are Serbs, while the citizens of Montenegro are Montenegrins. Ethnically, the answer is less clear. Terms such as Serb, Montenegrin, Albanian, and Croatian are national/political labels as well as ethnic identifiers. Others, such as Bosniak and Roma, are specific ethnic labels. In any event, determining one's identity is as much a matter of family history, religion, and language as it is of DNA.

The Kingdom of Serbs, Croats, and Slovenes, formed in 1918, was named for the main ethnicities of its subjects. When it changed its name to Yugoslavia in 1929, one of the most striking features was the great mixing of peoples. This mixing was a source of great cultural richness and diversity, but this diversity also tore the country apart, especially in the late 20th century.

This ethnic and religious diversity has been the product of both history and geography. Century after century, from the time of the ancient Romans, groups migrated into the area from Asia, the Middle East, the

Mediterranean lands, and other parts of Europe. Each group brought its own language, religion, and customs. Once a group had settled in an area, geography came into play, as settlements became isolated from one another by the rugged mountains and deep canyons.

The isolation helped people resist the power of outside invaders and develop a strong sense of independence. It also ensured that over many generations, the beliefs and customs of the culture would become deeply ingrained. Then, when others moved into the same area or conquered it, elements of the original culture would survive rather than be submerged.

After the death of Tito in 1980, Yugoslavia began to break apart along ethnic lines. Serbia, under Milosevic, led various efforts to unite ethnic Serbs into a "Greater Serbia." All such efforts failed and led to a great loss of life.

THE ETHNIC MIX

Two young women are dressed in Serbian national costumes for a folk dance in Belgrade.

The so-called barbarian invasions that continued from about the 3rd century CE through the 10th century brought a great variety of tribal groups into the region that became Yugoslavia. By the 600s, the earlier barbarian groups, such as the Goths, Huns, and Avars, had moved farther west, and a number of South Slavic tribes, including Serbs and Croatians, had come to dominate the region. While these tribal groups shared many physical characteristics and elements of culture, they were often at war with each other. From about 800 CE, the Serbs controlled much of the region.

Today in Serbia, ethnic Serbs make up about 83 percent of the population. Around 3.5 percent are Hungarians. Even smaller segments are Roma, Bosniaks, or Albanians. The figures are hard to pinpoint, however, because they are based on the 2011 census, which was boycotted by large numbers of Albanians. As a result, only 5,809 Albanians were recorded as living in Serbia, which is certainly not accurate. In the 2002 census, 61,647 Albanians were counted.

In Montenegro, the ethnic mix is a bit different. About 45 percent identify as ethnic Montenegrins, 28.7 percent as Serbs, 8.7 percent as Bosniaks, 4.9 percent as Albanians, and smaller percentages as Roma, Croatian, or other.

THE RELIGIOUS AND CULTURAL MIX

Conquest of the region by powerful empires added a variety of peoples and cultures, as well as religions. From the 8th century to the 14th, for example, the Byzantine Empire conquered nearly the entire Balkan region. The Byzantines brought a highly refined culture to the Slavic populations. It included outstanding architecture, art, and literature.

The Byzantine Empire introduced the Eastern Orthodox Church to the Slavs. To help the Slavic people read and understand the Bible, two monks—Cyril and Methodius—devised the alphabet that came to be known as Cyrillic.

Then, the Ottoman Turks, who were Muslims, moved into the area as the Byzantine Empire declined, conquering most of the Balkans by the 1400s. This empire brought with it its own culture and religion.

Children dress in Montenegrin national costumes at a folklore festival.

The population makeup of Serbia and Montenegro reflects the influence of both the Byzantine Empire and Ottoman Empire. In Serbia, about 85 percent of the people belong to the Serbian Orthodox Church, a branch of Eastern Orthodoxy. Only 5 percent are Roman Catholic, and 3 percent are Muslim. In Montenegro, Muslims make up a greater proportion of the population, at 19 percent. As in Serbia, the majority of the Montenegrin people are Eastern Orthodox Christians. Most belong to the Serbian Orthodox Church, though a small number have broken off and formed the outlier Montenegrin Orthodox Church.

The mixture of ethnic groups and religions in both countries has many regional variations. For instance, in an area that straddles the border between Serbia and Montenegro, a majority of the people are Bosniaks—Muslims who

FORMER YUGOSLAVIA

The countries of the former Yugoslavia are shown on this map, along with their national flags. In 2019, Macedonia changed its name to North Macedonia. Note that this map shows Kosovo in the same color as Serbia but has a border around it.

speak the Serbo-Croatian language but write it with the Latin alphabet, not the Cyrillic. The Serbian province of Vojvodina is also multiethnic. While about half the people are Serbs, the other half of the people include Hungarians, Croatians, Slovenes, Romanians (Vlads), and many other nationalities.

NATIONALISM AND ETHNIC TENSIONS

Nationalism has normally been a force that unites people as they strive to create a nation-state. In the Balkans, however, the land is divided among so many different groups that their nationalistic ambitions often collide.

For several centuries, the various groups lived in peace. Ethnic Serbs lived in the same towns or urban neighborhoods as Bosniaks, Croatians, and Slovenes. However, nationalist dreams began to emerge in the 1700s, becoming a powerful driving force in the 1800s and 1900s. People were now willing to fight and to die for this ideal of a nation.

When Yugoslavia was formed in 1918 (first as the Kingdom of Serbs, Croats, and Slovenes), it did not really answer the strong nationalist ambitions of the different groups. Later, when Marshal Tito reorganized Yugoslavia after World War II, he included six republics in an effort to satisfy those ambitions: Serbia, Croatia, Slovenia, Bosnia-Herzegovina, Montenegro, and Macedonia, plus the two autonomous provinces of Kosovo and Vojvodina. One reason that this arrangement was not more successful was that Serbia, the largest of the republics, tended to dominate the government. People in the other republics resented the Serb power and often feared that their republic would be swallowed up. The Serbs, in turn, were uneasy about border areas, where a local minority of Bosniaks or Croatians might want to join a neighboring republic.

While Tito's government managed to maintain peace and stability, the force of nationalism again became dominant in the 1990s. First the Slovenes, then the Croatians pulled away, followed by Bosnia and Herzegovina, and Macedonia. More trouble erupted when the people of Kosovo, nine-tenths of whom were ethnic Albanians, took up arms rather than yield to the power abuses of the Serbian police and military.

ETHNIC REFUGEES

The warfare of the 1990s displaced more than 2 million people. In the mid-1990s, for example, an estimated 640,000 refugees fled to Serbia from Croatia and Bosnia. Then, during the fighting in Kosovo in 1998 and 1999, another

In 2015, yet another huge wave of migrants passed through the Balkans. It included people escaping wartorn Syria. Here, Syrian refugees in the town of Berkasovo, Serbia, pass by a sign announcing the border of Croatia and Serbia.

600,000 people were on the move, and this time the refugees were mostly ethnic Albanians who fled to Albania, Macedonia, or Montenegro. When the NATO peacekeeping force moved in, the refugees began to return.

Once the NATO force had taken control of Kosovo, they ordered all Serbian government workers and police to leave the province. The Serb civilians who remained found that resentment against them was so strong that they no longer felt safe or comfortable living there. At the start of the 21st century, an estimated 200,000 Serb refugees from Kosovo had relocated to Belgrade or the province of Vojvodina.

TWO SPECIAL MINORITIES

Two small minority groups—the Roma, or Romani, who are the people formerly known as Gypsies, and the Jews—suffered terribly in World War II. Thousands of these people in then-Yugoslavia were rounded up by Nazi troops and by the Croatian pro-Nazi Ustasa and shipped to Nazi death camps. Only a few thousand of those who survived the war decided to remain in Yugoslavia.

A Roma family poses for a photo in Pancevo, Serbia.

The Roma of the Balkan Peninsula may have numbered 1 million people in 1939, when World War II began. Almost half that number—an estimated 400,000—died in Nazi labor camps and gas chambers.

The Roma were originally from northern India, and it is believed they migrated to the West in the 1100s, spreading throughout Europe. The few thousand who remain in Serbia and Montenegro continue to live on the fringes of society as fortune-tellers, circus performers, horse traders, day laborers, and jewelry makers.

There were around 33,000 Jews living in Serbia before World War II, mostly in Belgrade and Vojvodina. About two-thirds of them were murdered in the Holocaust. Most of those who survived left the country after the war, and very few Jews remain today in Serbia or Montenegro.

INTERNET LINKS

https://balkaninsight.com/2019/10/24/too-late-to-halt-serbias-demographic-disaster
This article about Serbia's population numbers gives up-to-date demographic information.

https://knoema.com/atlas/Montenegro
This site provides demographic statistics for Montenegro.

http://www.serbia.com/about-serbia/serbian-people
This site offers a section about the Serbian people, including famous people.

LIFESTYLE

The Central Square in Novi Sad, Serbia, glows at night. The monument is a sculpture of Svetozar Miletic, a 19-century mayor of the town.

7

THE PEOPLE OF MONTENEGRO AND Serbia live typical European lifestyles. Generally speaking, people in urban areas tend to live busier lives, with more cultural, shopping, and employment possibilities, as well as up-to-date transportation systems. People in rural regions, on the other hand, live quieter, more traditional lives. Throughout most of its history, the Yugoslavia region was primarily rural and agricultural. Cities and towns had existed since Roman times, but they remained small and contained only a fraction of the population.

Industry began to develop in the 20th century, especially after the Communist Party took control in 1945. The needs of industry led to a steady migration of people from farms to cities and towns. Still, by 1980, only about one-third of the population lived in urban areas.

At the beginning of the 21st century, that figure reached 52 percent, meaning that for the first time, more than half the people lived in cities and towns. Although the process of urbanization and industrialization had been slowed by the years of war, the change in lifestyle from rural

Novi Sad, Serbia, is one of three European Capitals of Culture for the year 2021. This prestigious designation is bestowed by the European Union on cities that exemplify the richness and diversity of European culture. (EU membership is not a factor.) The chosen cities use the opportunity to develop their cultural and creative potential so as to enable urban regeneration, improve their international image, and boost tourism.

to urban had started to speed up again. By 2019, 56.3 percent of Serbia's population and 67.2 percent of Montenegro's population lived in urban areas.

RURAL LIFE

In rural areas, life is slower, and people are more conservative, or traditional, in their tastes and values. In clothing styles, for example, many rural women now wear Western-style clothing, but some prefer their national costume—that is, the traditional outfit of an ethnic group or a geographic region.

These styles differ from region to region. Rural Serbian women wear ankle-length dresses covered by a short apron decorated with embroidery; they also wear heavy gold jewelry and head scarves that hang down in back. In Muslim villages, women usually wear baggy trousers gathered at the ankles and aprons embroidered in rich and vibrant colors. In city areas, these traditional styles are usually worn only on festive occasions.

This photo shows typical red-roofed homes in a rural Serbian village.

The way of life in rural areas also differs a good deal from region to region. The province of Vojvodina, for example, is located on the broad Pannonian Plain—a fertile land crisscrossed by rivers, making it the country's best farmland. The farms are large and generally prosperous, with broad fields of grains such as wheat and oats, along with orchards of plums and apples, as well as grapevines for making wine.

Villages in Vojvodina are generally large and far apart. Some larger towns, with between 5,000 and 10,000 people, are big enough to be considered urban, but they remain basically rural, serving the marketing and distribution needs of several farm villages. Some clusters of homes are surrounded by a wall or fence, often with a very ornate gate leading to a central courtyard, which provides some privacy.

In the hilly regions of Serbia, small farm villages appear along the roads that follow the crests of hills. The houses, built close together, are mostly constructed of logs or rough-hewn planks. They have shingle roofs and often plaster walls.

URBAN LIFE

City life also shows regional variations. Novi Sad is a university town in the province of Vojvodina that seems open, friendly, and proud of the diversity of its people. Roughly 20 percent are Hungarian, and there are reported to be 100 different national and ethnic groups in the city—Croatians, Slovenes, Bosniaks, Macedonians, Greeks, Bulgarians, and so on. Radio Novi Sad broadcasts in Serbian, Hungarian, Slovakian, and Romanian.

Novi Sad is a picturesque city nestled in a curve of the Danube, its ancient buildings and tiled roofs giving it the feeling of a medieval town. On weekends and in the evenings, couples and families stroll along the walls of the Petrovaradin Citadel, an elegant fortress built in the 1800s. It is also an important port on the busy Danube, transporting goods to Budapest, Hungary, and beyond.

Budva, on the Adriatic, is a Montenegrin beach resort with a more relaxed lifestyle. Its "Old Town" section was almost totally demolished in a 1979 earthquake, but it has been rebuilt with painstaking care. The town square, the churches, and the fortress all have the picturesque appearance of a movie set, drawing tourists back to the coast.

A few miles south of Budva is Sveti Stefan, which was once a small fishing village. The old stone cottages, with red tile roofs, are now available as luxurious rentals. Cetinje (set-IN-yeh), once the capital of Montenegro, has the aura of a citadel, which in fact it was—an impregnable fortress-city that resisted the armies of the Ottoman Turks for 500 years. Residents and visitors enjoy the narrow winding streets and the romantic old buildings.

LIFE IN BELGRADE

Belgrade is the capital of Serbia and by far its largest city, with about 1.4 million people. The city is an intriguing combination of the very old and the new, a city of fascinating images, such as a sleek Italian sports car parked in front of a thousand-year-old Eastern Orthodox church, or the glass wall of a modern

The historic center of Belgrade rises on the banks of the Sava River.

office building reflecting Kalemegdan Citadel, a solid 17th-century fortress looming over the "Old Town" section of the city.

The Old Town itself, a neighborhood called Stari Grad, is testimony to Belgrade's long history. The city dates back to the Illyrians in the fourth century BCE, and in its 2,500 years, it has been destroyed and rebuilt more than 40 times. Serbs are proud of their history, and many enjoy pointing out evidence of that history, such as a medieval gate, the tomb of a Muslim ruler, or Turkish public baths built in the 1500s.

A family enjoys the beautiful mountain view in Durmitor National Park in Montenegro.

Downtown Belgrade bustles with activity, with traffic jams and sidewalks crowded with office workers, shoppers, and tourists. The busy center of the city is Knez Mihailova—a pedestrian boulevard lined with stores, coffee shops, and cafés with outdoor tables. Businesspeople discuss deals while sipping thick Turkish coffee, and well-dressed patrons fill expensive restaurants, giving the city a sophisticated air not unlike Paris or Rome. Across the Sava River from downtown is "New Belgrade," an area of newer government buildings and apartment complexes.

FAMILY

The people of Serbia and Montenegro have a strong sense of family. Patterns of kinship, or extended family, are important in many areas of life. At weddings and other family gatherings, an individual is likely to see 40 or 50 family members—aunts, uncles, cousins, and so on. Someone seeking a job will mention family ties, and this can be a decisive factor. A custom called *kumstvo* (KUM-stvo) is also common. This is a form of family sponsorship, something like godparenthood, with informal ties that continue through a person's life.

In some regions, especially in Montenegro, people live in large family groups or clans. Relationships are close and intense. Usually these close-knit families enable children to grow up with a strong sense of security. One negative aspect

Students take a high school exam in Belgrade.

of clan life is that an insult to a clan member can fester for years and can sometimes lead to feuds that continue for generations.

EDUCATION

Schooling in both countries is free and compulsory for children beginning with preschool. Eight years of primary school and four years of secondary school follow, leading to a high school diploma. Beginning in the 2009 to 2010 school year, students no longer had to buy their textbooks, as all were provided for free, as long as they were returned at the end of the school year. In 2017, both Montenegro and Serbia had close to a 99 percent literacy rate.

In 2011, Serbia began offering adult education under the "Second Chance" program. These courses are offered to adults who never finished their education as children. They also help individuals—many of them Roma—who were never enrolled in primary school in the first place.

There are several universities in Serbia and Montenegro. Serbia has 17 universities, of which 8 are public and 9 are private, 63 colleges of applied sciences, of which 47 are public and 17 are private, and 8 colleges of academic studies, of which 3 are public and 5 are private. The University of Belgrade, founded in 1863, is the oldest; other state institutions of higher education are located in Kragujevac, Novi Sad, Nis, and Novi Pazar. Private schools are primarily located in Belgrade and Novi Sad. In Montenegro, the state-run University of Montenegro is in Podgorica; other private universities are also located in the city.

INTERNET LINKS

https://eacea.ec.europa.eu/national-policies/eurydice/content/montenegro_en
https://eacea.ec.europa.eu/national-policies/eurydice/content/serbia_en
The EU's European Commission hosts this site, which provides overviews of the Montenegrin and Serbian educational systems.

http://www.in-formality.com/wiki/index.php?title=Kumstvo_(Montenegro)
This article explains the *kumstvo* relationship in Montenegro.

http://uis.unesco.org/en/country/me
http://uis.unesco.org/en/country/rs
Statistics relating to education and literacy in Montenegro (/me) and Serbia (/rs) are available on these UNESCO pages.

RELIGION

The small Orthodox church of Sveti Luka (Saint Luke) in the Old Town of Kotor, Montenegro, dates to 1195.

8

FREEDOM OF RELIGION IS ENSHRINED in the constitutions of both Serbia and Montenegro. Neither country has a state religion. Discrimination against individuals because of their religion is illegal. In Serbia, however, the government does provide special treatment for seven religious groups it considers "traditional"—the Serbian Orthodox Church, Roman Catholic Church, Slovak Evangelical Church, Reformed Christian Church, Evangelical Christian Church, Islamic community, and Jewish community. These groups receive a tax break that other religious groups do not enjoy.

Religion has been a powerful force in the history of Europe—sometimes as a unifying force, but other times as a very divisive one. For some people, it plays more of a cultural role than a spiritual one, and most Serbs and Montenegrins don't practice their religion with great devotion. One study found that only about 10 percent of the people attend their church or mosque regularly. Older people, especially in rural areas, appear to be much more devout than most younger citizens.

During the Yugoslav years, the Communist Party government was hostile toward organized religion at first, but it then became more tolerant. The rise of strong nationalistic feelings in the 1980s and 1990s created a new interest in religion, and this is when it most recently proved to be both a unifying and a discordant force. Religion unified when it supported nationalistic hopes and dreams.

CATHOLIC AND ORTHODOX CHURCHES

The Eastern Orthodox Church and the Roman Catholic Church were originally the two main branches of Christianity. When the Roman Empire was divided into West (still called the Roman Empire) and East, the Eastern half became known as the Byzantine Empire, with its capital at Constantinople (today's Istanbul in Turkey).

In the centuries that followed, the two churches steadily grew farther apart. The pope in Rome is the head of the Roman Catholic Church. In the East, the bishop, or patriarch, of Constantinople leads the Eastern Orthodox

The impressive, large, white Church of St. Sava is a landmark building in Belgrade.

Church, though, in practice, each national church has exercised a good deal of independence. This independence is reflected in the names of some national churches, such as the Serbian Orthodox Church, the Greek Orthodox Church, and the Russian Orthodox Church.

The service of the Eastern Orthodox Church also developed in different ways. It's a very elaborate service, with a strong appeal to the senses through the haunting chants of the music, the heavy smell of incense, and the visual image of many icons (paintings of religious figures, such as the saints and the holy family).

THE APOSTLES OF THE SLAVS

Two brothers played an important part in the development of both the religion and language of the Yugoslav region. Both Cyril and Methodius were brilliant scholars, specializing in theology and language. In 863, the patriarch of Constantinople sent them to convert the Slavic tribes to Christianity. In order to teach the Holy Scriptures (the Bible), they used the Slavonic language.

The Cathedral of Saint Tryphon in Kotor is one of two Roman Catholic cathedrals in Montenegro.

Since there was no written form of the language, the brothers invented an alphabet, built on Slavonic sounds and based on the Greek alphabet. This alphabet, called Cyrillic, is still used in Serbia, North Macedonia, Russia, and several other countries. Originally, the Cyrillic alphabet required 43 characters to cover the variations of Slavonic sounds, but modifications have reduced the number to 30 letters (32 in Russia).

For their great contributions, the brothers became known as the Apostles of the Slavs, and they were made saints in both the Catholic and Orthodox Churches. Their feast day is celebrated on February 14 in the Roman Catholic Church and May 11 in the Eastern Orthodox Church.

MAJORITY AND MINORITY RELIGIONS

The larger Yugoslavia was a great mixture of religious, ethnic, and linguistic groups. In the six constituent republics, Roman Catholics formed the largest group in Croatia and Slovenia; Muslims were a majority in Bosnia and Herzegovina; and the Eastern Orthodox religion was dominant in Serbia, Montenegro, and Macedonia.

In Serbia, almost 85 percent of the people are Eastern Orthodox, about 5 percent are Roman Catholic, and 3 percent are Muslim. In Montenegro, the majority is also Orthodox, but Muslims make up a larger portion of the population—72 percent are Orthodox, 19 percent are Muslim, and 3.4 percent are Roman Catholic. In both countries, the remaining few are Protestants, atheists, or members of other religions.

THE EASTERN ORTHODOX CHURCH AND NATIONALISM

During the five centuries of Turkish Ottoman (Muslim) rule, some Serbs converted to Islam because they knew that they would have greater opportunities in business and government as Muslims. Those who remained in the Eastern Orthodox Church were exposed to discrimination. Some expressions of prejudice were merely nuisances. For instance, when a Muslim

THE OSTROG MONASTERY

The gleaming white church of the Ostrog Monastery perches nearly 3,000 feet (900 m) up on a vertical cliffside in Ostroska Greda, Montenegro. It appears to have been carved out of a solid wall of rock, but it was actually built into a cave. Dedicated to Saint Vasilije (Basil) of Ostrog, the monastery is sometimes dubbed "Saint Vasilije's miracle" because its very existence seems miraculous.

Founded by Vasilije, a bishop of Herzegovina, in the 17th century, the monastery is still active today, a part of the Serbian Orthodox Church. The complex is made up of an upper and lower monastery. The upper building houses two churches; one holds the enshrined remains of Saint Vasilije, and both feature impressive frescoes on their walls and rock walls. The lower building, built in 1824, houses a third church and most of the monks' living quarters.

The site attracts up to a million visitors and religious pilgrims each year. The scenic view from the steep rock face is extraordinary in itself, but it is also a site of holy devotion for many faithful. Pilgrims traditionally walk the 1.9-mile (3 km) path from the lower monastery to the upper monastery barefoot.

rode by on horseback, a Serb rider was expected to dismount and wait for the rider to pass. Other manifestations of prejudice were more troublesome, such as paying higher taxes or being forbidden to live in certain neighborhoods.

Centuries later, during the civil war of the 1990s, Serb soldiers inflicted grim revenge on the Muslim Bosniaks who became their prisoners. They felt it was a justified payback for the humiliation inflicted on their families by the Ottoman Turks—an indication of the depth of ethnic bitterness.

For most Serbs and Montenegrins, the Eastern Orthodox Church was a safe haven and a source of strength during the years of Turkish rule, from 1389 to 1878. The church enabled people to retain their national identity. They held secret meetings in the churches and even planned armed uprisings against the occupying armies.

The clandestine meetings helped the tough fighters of Montenegro avoid a complete Turkish conquest. From 1482, Montenegro was ruled from Cetinje by leaders called *vladike* (vla-DEE-ke)—bishops in the Eastern Orthodox Church. Today, Cetinje is considered the Old Royal Capital of Montenegro.

RELIGION IN MONTENEGRO

Most Montenegrins are Eastern Orthodox Christians, but within that religion are various denominations. Having once been part of the larger Yugoslavia, and then Serbia-Montenegro, the country still has a sizable number of people who belong to the Serbian Orthodox Church. For them, the incredible 17th-century Ostrog Monastery is one of Montenegro's primary religious landmarks and the most popular pilgrimage site.

Just as Christianity was broken in two by the East-West schism a thousand years ago, today's Orthodox Church is beset by schisms. Breakaway churches that claim to represent "true" orthodox theology are called autocephalous (independent) and noncanonical. They are not recognized by the patriarch of Constantinople. A subset of Orthodox Christians in Montenegro belongs to one such church, the Montenegrin Orthodox Church. (Others include the Ukrainian Autocephalous Orthodox Church and the Macedonian Orthodox Church.)

Most Roman Catholics in Montenegro are ethnic Albanians or Croatians. Among the Muslims in the country are ethnic Slavs and ethnic Albanians. The Slavic Muslims are largely Bosnian-speaking Bosniaks and Albanian Muslims. Islam is the dominant religion in Montenegro's northeastern municipalities.

ISLAM

Muslims are followers of Islam. Islam is considered one of the world's great religions, founded by the Prophet Muhammad in the seventh century CE. It is a monotheistic religion, meaning followers believe in a single god, and Muslims accept some portions of both Judaism and Christianity. Muslims, for example, accept the biblical Abraham, Moses, and Jesus as great prophets, but Muhammad is considered the final and greatest of the prophets.

The Five Pillars of Islam, rules to be followed by the faithful, include answering the five daily calls to prayer. The call is given by someone called a muezzin, usually from a tower called a minaret. In Muslim neighborhoods, prayer takes place in a mosque. If a mosque is not available, Muslims kneel wherever they can on a small prayer rug facing the holy city of Mecca (in Saudi Arabia). Another of the Five Pillars is to observe the holy month of Ramadan by fasting and praying each day of the month from dawn to sunset.

For centuries, the Balkan people of the various religions coexisted. In fact, in many towns and cities, Roman Catholics, Eastern Orthodox Christians, and Muslims were proud of the diversity, often sharing the same neighborhood. The powerful force of nationalism unleashed the submerged fears and resentment that had lurked beneath the surface, and the resulting explosion of hatred was sometimes expressed in terms of religion. However, many people are working to create a sense of peace among the different groups once again.

INTERNET LINKS

https://me.usembassy.gov/wp-content/uploads/sites/250/ MONTENEGRO-2018-INTERNATIONAL-RELIGIOUS-FREEDOM -REPORT.pdf
https://rs.usembassy.gov/wp-content/uploads/sites/235/Serbia -2018-International-Religious-Freedom-Report.pdf
These are US State Department reports on religious freedom in both countries.

http://www.serbia.com/visit-serbia/cultural-attractions/ monasteries-and-churches
Some of the most important monasteries and churches in Serbia are profiled on this site.

https://theculturetrip.com/europe/serbia/articles/a-guide-to -religions-in-serbia
This site provides an overview of religion in Serbia.

LANGUAGE

A monument to Saints Cyril and Methodius in Belgrade
celebrates the literacy of the Slavic people.

МЕТОДИЈЕ

9

THE PEOPLE WHO SETTLED IN WHAT would become the Yugoslav region were Slavic. The diversity that emerged was based on religion and language rather than on different physical characteristics. The people of both Montenegro and Serbia mostly belong to the Eastern Orthodox Church, while most Bosnians are Muslims and Croatians are largely Roman Catholics. The language of all four nations is Serbo-Croatian, although in Serbia, the language is officially called Serbian. A more important distinction is that Serbs use the Cyrillic alphabet, while Croatians use the Roman alphabet.

THE BEGINNING OF AN ALPHABET

In 863 CE, two Greek brothers—Cyril and Methodius—were sent to the Slavic lands by the patriarch of the Eastern Orthodox Church. The two monks were brilliant scholars and linguists, and their mission was to Christianize the southern Slavs. To acquaint the Slavic-speaking peoples with the Bible, they invented an alphabet, now called Cyrillic, based on

In December 2017, Montenegrin was officially recognized by the International Organization for Standardization as a separate language from Serbian. The National Library of Montenegro had lobbied for this for nine years, adding two letters to the Montenegrin alphabet, in both Latin and Cyrillic, to differentiate it from Serbian. However, the two languages remain essentially the same.

Both the Latin and Cyrillic alphabets can be seen in the various newspapers at a stand in Belgrade.

the Greek alphabet. Since Slavic languages were rich in sounds, the brothers found they needed 43 letters, a number that has since been reduced.

The brothers were made saints in both the Eastern Orthodox and Roman Catholic branches of Christianity for Christianizing many Slavic peoples and for influencing the cultural development of those peoples. Together, Saint Cyril and Saint Methodius have the title of the Apostles of the Slavs.

LANGUAGE VARIATIONS

The division between the Croatian and Serbian languages originated in the 11th century when both groups converted to Christianity. The Serbs were aligned with the Eastern Orthodox Church, which used the Cyrillic alphabet. The Croatians followed the Roman Catholic Church and its use of the Latin alphabet. In the 19th century, Vuk Stefanovic Karadzic simplified the Serbian written language.

LANGUAGE REFORMER

Vuk Stefanovic Karadzic (1787–1864) was both a hero of Serb nationalism and a brilliant scholar who improved and simplified the Serbian language. In addition, he was the country's greatest collector of folk songs and stories.

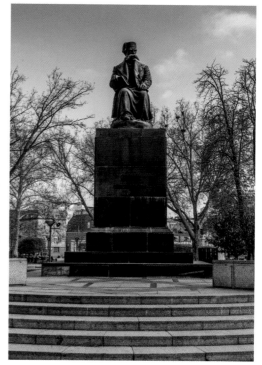

As a Serbian patriot, Karadzic took part in the first uprising against the Ottoman Turks, in 1804. One of his duties was to read and write for the Serb commanders, most of whom were illiterate. After several years of revolution, he was forced to flee. He went to Vienna, Austria, where he became known as an outstanding scholar.

Karadzic began collecting popular songs and poems, but he was troubled by inconsistencies in the Cyrillic script, especially a duplication of sounds. He discovered that the Serbian language contained 30 sounds, but the Cyrillic alphabet had no letters for 6 of them.

He created new symbols and discarded 18 others that were not needed. In 1818, he published his Serbian Lexicon (Srpski Rjecnik),

A monument to Vuk Stefanovic Karadzic stands in Belgrade.

which was updated in 1852 to more than 46,000 words. Many church officials objected to the drastic changes, but the new alphabet was so simple and effective that the opposition soon disappeared. The lexicon (dictionary), which includes valuable information about folklore, is still considered a classic.

In most areas of Serbia and Montenegro, the majority of people are Slavs who speak the Serbian language and use the Cyrillic alphabet. However, there are some regional variations. Near Serbia's border with Bosnia and Herzegovina, for example, the majority of the people are Bosniaks. They speak the Serbian language, but they usually call it Serbo-Croatian, and they write it in the Roman (or Latin) script.

SOME SAMPLE WORDS AND PHRASES

English	Serbian	Pronounced
hello	zdravo	*ZDRAH-vo*
good-bye	dovidjenja	*doh-vee-DYEH-nyah*
yes	da	*DAH*
no	ne	*NEH*
please	molim	*MOH-leem*
thank you	hvala	*HVAH-lah*
excuse me (sorry)	oprostite	*OH-proh-steet*
What's your name?	Kako se zovete?	*KAH-koh SEH ZOO-veht-eh?*
My name is …	Zovem se …	*ZOH-vehm SEH*
Do you speak English?	Govorite li Engleski?	*GO-vor-ee-the LEE ehn-GLEH-skee*
Where is …	Gde je …	*GDEH YEH*
one	jedan	*YEH-dahn*
ten	deset	*DEH-seht*
twenty	dvadeset	*DVAH-deh-seht*

Ethnic Albanians form a majority in several areas of the disputed territory of Kosovo, formerly an autonomous province of Serbia. Most of these people are Muslims, but to add to the confusion, large numbers are Orthodox Christians and smaller numbers are Roman Catholic. All speak Albanian and use the Roman alphabet.

In the autonomous province of Vojvodina, Hungarians are a majority in a number of towns and villages. Most speak both Hungarian and Serbian; many use the Latin alphabet, although they are able to read the Cyrillic script, at least for such practical things as street signs.

Most people in Serbia and Montenegro have at least a casual knowledge of a second language. For many, that language is German, a legacy of the 1970s and 1980s, when thousands of Yugoslav workers lived temporarily in West Germany, where the economy was successful and the workers could send most of their earnings home to what was then Yugoslavia. English is also a popular second language, especially among young people.

PRONUNCIATION

The writing systems of Serbian are phonetic—that is, every letter is pronounced, and the sound represented by that letter does not change from word to word. There is some variation in where the stress is placed in a word, but the one general rule is that the stress, or accent, is never on the last syllable, and in most words it is on the first vowel.

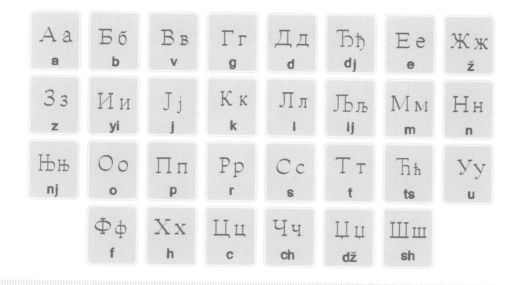

А а	Б б	В в	Г г	Д д	Ђ ђ	Е е	Ж ж
a	b	v	g	d	dj	e	ž

З з	И и	Ј ј	К к	Л л	Љ љ	М м	Н н
z	yi	j	k	l	lj	m	n

Њ њ	О о	П п	Р р	С с	Т т	Ћ ћ	У у
nj	o	p	r	s	t	ts	u

Ф ф	Х х	Ц ц	Ч ч	Џ џ	Ш ш
f	h	c	ch	dž	sh

INTERNET LINKS

https://inserbia.info/what-language-is-spoken-in-serbia
Language use in Serbia is covered on this site.

https://www.omniglot.com/writing/montenegrin.htm#
https://www.omniglot.com/writing/serbian.htm
These are introductions to the Montenegrin and Serbian languages.

https://theculturetrip.com/europe/montenegro/articles/
21-essential-phrases-youll-need-in-montenegro
This travel site provides common phrases in Montenegrin.

ARTS

In Podgorica, this monument celebrates the
oro, the Montenegrin national dance.

10

THE ARTS IN SERBIA AND Montenegro reflect the countries' history, religion, values, and geography. They express the long folk history of the people and of the different ethnic and religious groups. Modern music and dance draw on the folk arts of the past. Literature and poetry build on historic themes, exploring centuries of warfare waged against the Turks, then the Austrians and Hungarians, and then the Germans in World War II— conflicts that often ended in tragedy.

Another influence on the arts has been the Eastern Orthodox Church. It had a particularly strong impact on the early development of the arts. From about 1000 to 1400 CE, the architecture and decorations of the churches represented outstanding contributions to art. Poetry and painting also dealt with religious themes, at least until influences from Western Europe began to be felt in the mid-1800s. These later influences involved first the Romantic era of heroic paintings and poetry, then the impressionism of the late 1800s.

The wars of the 20th century caused the destruction of many cultural monuments and artifacts. The Institute for the Protection of Cultural Monuments was created in 1947 to identify, study, and protect Serbia's "cultural property."

The *oro* is a popular folk dance, often performed at Orthodox wedding receptions in Montenegro. The name derives from the word for "eagle," as the movements are said to resemble those of the great bird. The double-headed eagle is also an important symbol in Eastern Orthodox imagery.

Just as UNESCO works to protect natural and cultural World Heritage sites, it also identifies examples of "intangible cultural heritage of humanity" that need to be preserved. These include, according to the group's website, "traditions or living expressions inherited from our ancestors and passed on to our descendants, such as oral traditions, performing arts, social practices, rituals, arts, festive events, knowledge and practices concerning nature and the universe or the knowledge and skills to produce traditional crafts."

The Convention for the Safeguarding of the Intangible Cultural Heritage has listed three entries for Serbia—the Slava, the celebration of a family patron saint's day; the kolo, *a traditional folk dance; and singing to the accompaniment of the gusle, a traditional, single-stringed instrument of the Balkans, shown below.*

Montenegro has none listed at this writing, but some may be added in the future.

RELIGION AND THE ARTS

The most famous artworks in Serbia and Montenegro are beautiful frescoes (wall paintings) produced in the 13th and 14th centuries in Orthodox churches scattered throughout the mountains and valleys. Ecclesiastical frescoes depicting scenes from the Bible and from the lives of the saints are among the great treasures of world art. The Studenica Monastery in central Serbia, which dates from 1190, is well known for its magnificent 13th- and 14th-century Byzantine-style frescoes. During the 14th century, when Serbia was under Ottoman occupation, the ruling Muslims banned the worship of idols (a principle doctrine of Islam) and scraped off most of the faces of the Christian saints painted on the walls. Today, Studenica is the largest and richest of Serbia's Orthodox monasteries, and the property is listed as a UNESCO World Heritage site.

One of the best known frescoes in Serbia is the so-called "White Angel" at the Mileseva Monastery in southwest Serbia. The picture is part of a much larger fresco composition, *Myrrhbearers on Christ's Grave*, on a wall in the monastery's Church of the Ascension of Christ. The luminous image is of an angel, dressed in white robes, sitting outside Christ's tomb and pointing to its empty interior to tell visitors (myrrhbearers) of Christ's resurrection. The fresco painter is unknown, and in the 16th century, the White Angel was painted over with another fresco. It was hidden until the 20th century, when the original fresco was restored. Today, it is considered one of the most beautiful examples of Serbian—and European—fresco art.

Another example of the lasting influence of the Orthodox Church is in medieval songs and chants. The Cetinje Monastery in Montenegro has one of Europe's oldest and largest collections of liturgical music. The pure and somewhat haunting sounds are still sung and recorded by choral groups from many parts of the world.

The "White Angel," a section of the fresco *Myrrhbearers on Christ's Grave*, is a famous work of art on the walls of the Mileseva Monastery in Serbia.

The renovated Museum of Contemporary Art in Belgrade collects and displays work produced since 1900 in Serbia and the former Yugoslavia.

MUSEUMS

Two of the most important art museums in Serbia were closed to the public for many years. In 2003, the National Museum of Serbia in Belgrade—arguably Serbia's premier museum—closed its doors for renovation. In 2007, the Museum of Contemporary Art, also in Belgrade, did the same. Both buildings were deteriorating, and their interiors were not up to international museum standards. During the war years of the 1990s, the museums had been neglected. However, once closed, the money and political will to do the necessary work in both institutions evidently evaporated.

The National Museum first opened in 1844, and in 1950, it moved into its present location, a monumental red brick building in Republic Square that was once a bank. The museum houses more than 400,000 objects of art and archaeology from ancient times to the 20th century. It includes around 6,000 works of Serbian and Yugoslav-era art, as well as more than 2,000 works from Europe, Russia, Japan, and China.

The Museum of Contemporary Art is housed in an impressively modern building built in 1965. Its collection includes 35,000 Serbian and Yugoslav works produced in the 20th and 21st centuries, and it has hosted international exhibitions of modern and contemporary art as well.

This aerial view shows the National Museum of Montenegro, a landmark in the city of Cetinje.

With both museums closed, and no reopening dates in sight, the Serbian people wondered if they would ever again be able to visit these exalted places. After all, at the time, the country was in great upheaval. Political figures were being murdered, and the prime minister had just been assassinated. Government concern for museum renovation understandably had to take a back seat for a while.

As the political situation in Serbia settled down, the government eventually realized that the museum situation had to be solved. As the country is seeking to join the European Union, it needed to bring its capital city up to European standards for culture. In October 2017, the Museum of Contemporary Art reopened after 10 years of renovation work. Nearly 50,000 art lovers showed up for the opening. In June 2018, the National Museum reopened after being closed for 15 years. The reopening ceremony for the National Museum included a children's choir and a video display on the building's facade.

Montenegro's top museums did not suffer such a setback. The Museum of Fine Arts in Cetinje, with collections of Montenegrin and Yugoslav art as well as international works, is part of the larger National Museum of Montenegro, which chronicles the history of the nation. It is the country's oldest and most respected institution. There are many other museums dotting the small country.

One of the great historical treasures of Eastern Europe is the Miroslav Gospel. This is the oldest known Cyrillic document in the region. Illustrated with detailed miniatures, the 362-page Gospel was created in the year 1186 at Saint Peter's Church in Bijelo Polje, a town in northeastern Montenegro. Both Montenegrins and Serbs claim the work as their own.

The priceless volume was nearly lost during World War I, when a Serb army unit, retreating to escape the advancing Austrian army, carried it in a saddlebag through the mountains of Greece. Several years later, it was returned from the island of Crete and presented to the king of Yugoslavia. It is now on display at the National Museum in Belgrade.

In 2005, the Miroslav Gospel was inscribed in UNESCO's Memory of the World Register in recognition of its historical value. This UNESCO listing is a compendium of documents, manuscripts, oral traditions, audio-visual materials, and library and archival holdings considered to be of universal value.

LITERATURE

Nationalist strivings of the Serbs and Montenegrins inspired the first great literary efforts in these countries. In 1847, Petar II Petrovic-Njegos, the bishop-prince of Montenegro, wrote an epic drama called *The Mountain Wreath* (*Gorski vijenac*) using the rhythms of folktales. Also in the 19th century, Vuk Karadzic collected examples of the South Slavic oral tradition—folk songs, poems, stories, and myths. His *Serbian Folk Poems* filled four volumes, and he also published a book of popular stories and a collection of Serbian proverbs. His collections are well known throughout Europe.

The World War II novels of Ivo Andric achieved international recognition. Of Andric's novels, *The Bridge on the Drina* (1945) is probably the best known, and he won the Nobel Prize for Literature in 1961—the only Yugoslav to achieve such an honor. His books are now regarded as classics, even though many Bosniak critics feel his writings were anti-Muslim.

Another writer who had political problems was Milovan Djilas of Montenegro. In the 1950s, while he was vice president of Yugoslavia, he began writing books that criticized the Communist Party government—a government that he had helped to create. His nonfiction book called *The New Class* (1957) was a harsh indictment of communism that cost him his political career. In spite of these difficulties, Djilas continued to write novels, histories, essays, and memoirs.

Contemporary Serbian literature is well represented by *The Cyclist Conspiracy* (2009) by the award-winning writer Svetislav Basara. It's one of the few works of this prolific author available in English.

A statue of author Ivo Andric stands at the entrance to Pioneer Park in central Belgrade.

One of the great writers of Serbia and Montenegro was Petar II Petrovic-Njegos (1813–1851). He belonged to a clan of hereditary leaders, and he became both a bishop of the Eastern Orthodox Church and a ruler of Montenegro. When his uncle died in 1830, he became the ruler at the age of 17, and he served until his untimely death in 1851.

Njegos, as he is commonly known, is best remembered today as an outstanding poet. His most famous poem, the epic Gorski vijenac (The Mountain Wreath), *is considered a masterpiece of Serbian and Montenegrin literature. Its main themes are the struggle for freedom, justice, and dignity, and resistance against Ottoman domination.*

Njegos is known for more than just the quality of his poetry, however. He, perhaps more than anyone, was responsible for romanticizing the nationalism inherent in what's called "the Kosovo Myth"—the story of the 1389 Battle of Kosovo that came to signify Serbian righteousness and patriotic glory. In The Mountain Wreath, *Njegos built on the myth's ethnocentricity by focusing on a little-known 18th-century encounter between Montenegrin Orthodox Christians and Slavic Muslims (who had converted to Islam under the centuries of Ottoman rule). The event culminated in a mass execution of Muslims on Orthodox Christmas Day, which the poem celebrates as a righteous vindication. The poem touches on themes that trace their roots to the original Kosovo myth, including betrayal, vengeance for the honor of the Montenegrin Serb nation, and the supremacy of European Christendom over the invading Muslim Turks.*

Njegos's works elevated these values in a way that established a sort of "origin myth" for the Serbian and Montenegrin people and a corresponding national identity. Over the years, Serbian nationalists, Yugoslavs, Communists—and notably, Slobodan Milosevic—have drawn inspiration from Njegos's works.

Today, the prince-poet's remains are interred in a mausoleum (shown here) on top of Mount Lovcen in southwestern Montenegro. In 2013, on the 200th anniversary of his birth, Njegos was named Montenegro's national poet—a controversial move that doesn't sit well with the nation's Muslim citizens.

MUSIC AND DANCE

Like all the arts, music and dance in Serbia and Montenegro reveal a strong folk tradition. Some of the music and dance is similar to that of neighboring Bulgaria, including the instruments used. The *gajde* (GEI-de), for example, which looks like an oversized set of bagpipes, provides a wailing background sound in many songs, including folk songs that date back more than a thousand years. Combined with flutes and fiddles, the gajde offers a surprising richness and variety. Accordions are also popular in Serbian folk music

Traditional folk songs from different regions also accompany folk-dance groups, each group wearing costumes and following traditional steps from their own colorful past. The kolo is the national dance, which is typically

Young Serbian dancers dressed in traditional costumes perform at an international folk festival in Romania.

performed in a circle. The kolo has been inscribed on UNESCO's Intangible Cultural Heritage List.

There are numerous variations on the folk traditions. Many people love the loud, brassy sounds of Balkan brass—best exemplified by Serbia's national brass band. This musical form is dominated by men, many of whom learned the music from their fathers. The brass music of Serbia has been heavily influenced by the brass bands of Turkey and Austria. If Serbia has a national music, this is it, and the annual Trumpet Festival of Guca brings in crowds of around 600,000 brass band fans.

Modern music is also part of the thriving music industry. For example, a type of music known as neofolk is especially popular among rural families and industrial workers, much like country rock in the United States. Serbian rock groups are consistently popular, and many have been active in social or political movements, such as the antiwar protests of the 1990s and the anti-Milosevic movement of 1999 to 2002. Many Serbian musicians express their political

A brass band plays as it marches in a parade at the music festival in Guca.

MILOS KARADAGLIC

One of Montenegro's biggest international stars is classical guitar player Milos Karadaglic. Born in 1983, the popular musician often goes by just the name Milos (MEE-lohsh). As a young man, he attended London's Royal Academy of Music, and he then began performing concerts. His breakout year was 2012, and he has since wowed audiences throughout Europe, North America, Asia, and Australia. Between 2011 and 2016, he released four albums. His repertoire includes classical works and pop favorites. In 2016, he released an album of Beatles songs.

A hand injury in 2016 set him back for more than a year, but he returned to performing in 2018. His latest release, as of early 2020, is the album Sound of Silence *(2019), which features solo guitar work, reimagined pop classics, and some jazz songs with guest artists.*

views through their music. Rap, hip-hop, punk, and metal groups produce their own regional superstars, as popular in the Balkans as any Western megastar.

Opera, ballet, and classical orchestral music continue to have a small but dedicated following that has persisted since the mid-1800s. Serbia and Montenegro's proximity to Vienna, a major center for traditional European performing arts, has influenced the love of those art forms.

FILM AND THEATER

Yugoslav filmmakers produced some of the best films of the entire communist world. This trend began in the closing months of World War II, when some experimental filmmakers began making documentaries about their war-torn land. They next turned to animated films and then to feature films. The tradition begun by these pioneers continues into the 21st century, and film remains an important medium for social and political commentary.

In 1971, Belgrade launched FEST, one of Eastern Europe's most important international film festivals. Since its founding, it has hosted more than 4 million visitors and screened around 4,000 relevant international films, many of which had their premiere at the festival. Originally noncompetitive, in 2015 FEST was transformed into an official competition festival with four distinct competition selections: "International Films;" "Serbian Films;" "Frontiers," featuring subversive, controversial, and art-house films; and the "Nebojsa Djukelic Award," a regional award named for a Serbian film critic.

Theater is also a vibrant part of Serbia's cultural life. The National Theatre in Belgrade is the center for live drama, with some plays produced in the language of Slovenia, in addition to those produced in Serbo-Croatian.

The National Theatre in Belgrade gleams on an evening in October 2019.

INTERNET LINKS

**https://classicalguitarmagazine.com/milos-karadaglic-returns
-after-a-devastating-hand-injury**
This music magazine conducts an in-depth interview with Montenegrin guitarist Milos Karadaglic.

**https://www.collectorsweekly.com/articles/why-brass-musicians
-cant-resist-serbias-wildest-festival**
This article paints a colorful picture of the Guca Trumpet Festival.

https://www.fest.rs
The home site of the FEST International Film Festival in Belgrade is posted in English.

https://ich.unesco.org/en/RL/kolo-traditional-folk-dance-01270
The UNESCO Intangible Cultural Heritage listing for the kolo dance is found on this page.

http://www.narodnimuzej.rs/?lang=en
This is the site of the National Museum in Belgrade.

http://www.serbia.com/about-serbia/culture
This site offers a wide-ranging section on Serbian literature, film, music, and intangible heritage.

**https://theculturetrip.com/europe/serbia/articles/the-10-most
-influential-serbian-artists-in-history**
This site provides a quick survey of great Serbian artists.

https://whc.unesco.org/en/list/389
This listing of the Studenica Monastery on the UNESCO World Heritage website includes photos and a video.

LEISURE

Boys kick a ball around after school in a park in Belgrade.

N GENERAL, SERBS AND
Montenegrins enjoy being outdoors.
Leisure activities range from vigorous
outdoor activities, such as hunting
and skiing, to quieter pastimes, such
as hiking. They also enjoy watching
movies or television, surfing the
internet, and playing cards. Young
people enjoy playing video games,
listening to loud rock and pop music, and
visiting the newest shopping malls.

Urban centers are characterized by traffic jams and sidewalks crowded with shoppers, office workers, and vacationers. Bright lights draw customers to shops, theaters, restaurants, and dance clubs, while the colorful umbrellas of sidewalk cafés burst open like spring blossoms whenever the sun shines.

HUNTING AND FISHING

The rugged mountains and sparkling streams of Serbia and Montenegro have lured hunters and fishers from all over the Balkans and the rest of Europe for 200 years or more. Many are drawn by big game such as the

Carpathian red deer, known for its large antlers; the swift and dangerous wild boar; and the big Bosnian brown bear. Many animal species that have become rare or extinct in other parts of Europe are still plentiful here. The same is true of game birds, including pheasant, grouse, and waterfowl.

Since the 1980s, amid rising concern for environmental conservation, there has been a new interest in hunting with binoculars and a camera rather than a rifle or shotgun. The marsh regions of Carska Bara and Obedska Bara offer more than 200 species of birds in fields carpeted with marsh wildflowers.

There are numerous fishing centers in Serbia and Montenegro. The many lakes, as well as rivers such as the Sava, Tisa, and Danube, offer an abundance of fish, including bass, carp, catfish, pike, sturgeon, trout, perch, and salmon. In Durmitor National Park, 18 crystal-clear lakes offer outstanding fishing, as do the region's mountain streams.

SPAS

Spas have a long tradition in Serbia and Montenegro. Most lie at the foot of a mountain, surrounded by forest. The mild climates, natural beauty, and therapeutic qualities of thermal mineral springs draw thousands of visitors annually. The Sokobanja spa tourist resort in Serbia is located between mountains. This area has been a tourist destination for 150 years. Montenegro also has a number of spas and wellness centers.

SEASONAL ACTIVITIES

Durmitor National Park in Montenegro is a favorite place for weekend getaways or vacations. Camping, hiking, fishing, and mountain climbing (mountaineering) are popular. Hikers enjoy trekking around the lakes. Even the largest, Crno Jezero, or Black Lake, is no more than a day's hike. On hot summer days, walking around a lake offers hikers the chance to cool off with a refreshing swim.

Black Lake is a deep turquoise in this aerial view of Durmitor National Park in Montenegro.

People enjoy a sunny day at Petrovac Beach in Budva on the coast of Montenegro.

Another feature of Durmitor is Tara Canyon, where the churning rapids of the Tara River offer a spectacular challenge to white-water rafters. Other swift rivers, such as some of the tributaries of the Danube, are inviting both to rafters and to hikers. Sailing races and other water-related events are held every summer on the Danube in cities like Belgrade and Novi Sad.

Montenegro's coastline has many beautiful beaches. The so-called Budvan Riviera surrounds the city of Budva, the Montenegrin center of culture and tourism. Budva's Old Town was destroyed in a 1979 earthquake and rebuilt as a tourist attraction.

Horseback riding is also popular, and every September the town of Pozarevac hosts an equestrian tournament at Ljubicevo, a famous horse farm and stable. Other summer sports include cycling, rock climbing, and paragliding.

Both Serbia and Montenegro are well known for winter sports. Serbia is best known for skiing, and the 26 runs at Kopaonik bring skiers from every corner of Europe. The same is true of Montenegro's winter resorts, such as Zabljak.

ENTERTAINMENT

Serbs and Montenegrins spend a good deal of their free time with their families. The midday meal is often a festive occasion, especially on weekends and holidays, when it is likely to include family stories, games, or dancing. Some families enjoy an evening in front of the television set, but most still prefer to go out for an evening walk. In the cities, such an evening stroll is often along the walls of a citadel or on a pedestrian boulevard from which motor vehicles have been excluded. These walks take people past a variety of architectural styles, some dating back many centuries.

Sidewalk cafés are a popular stop for a drink, such as one of the well-known regional wines or beers, Turkish coffee, or espresso. The night spots feature live music, ranging from traditional folk songs to jazz, rock, and even hip-hop.

In Belgrade, there is a stretch of more than 20 barges and boats docked on the Danube and Sava Rivers that are used for partying. The city has more

People enjoy city life at an outdoor café in Belgrade.

sophisticated entertainment as well, including the National Theatre, founded in the mid-1800s, and the Belgrade Philharmonic Orchestra.

Several cities and towns are restoring historic areas, recreating neighborhoods centered on relaxation and enjoyment. In Belgrade, for example, Skadarska Street now has rebuilt cobblestone pedestrian walkways and features strolling musicians in folk costumes and a variety of shops and cafés.

For many, leisure activities involve simple pleasures. This is particularly true for people living in rural areas. In fact, tourists from other parts of Europe have recently become attracted to the idea of staying with a rural family, perhaps engaging in a little farmwork and then enjoying hikes through meadows blanketed with wildflowers or into the mountains.

SPORTS

The people of Serbia and Montenegro engage in a wide range of both individual and team sports. Soccer is immensely popular in both countries, and the original Yugoslavia fielded excellent national teams in the competition for the World Cup—the most popular sports event in the world. Amateur and professional teams are active throughout both countries, and many local clubs compete in semiprofessional leagues.

Perhaps Serbia's greatest sports hero today is pro tennis superstar Novak Djokovic. In January 2020, he entered the Australian Open as the reigning champion and was ranked Number 2 in the world in men's singles. He had at that point accumulated 16 Grand Slam titles—only the third man ever to do so, after Switzerland's Roger Federer and Spain's Rafael Nadal.

However, soccer remains the favorite spectator sport, and every city has a stadium, usually filled to capacity for matches between professional teams. The stadiums are also used for track-and-field events, and indoor auditoriums are used for events such as boxing, wrestling, weight lifting, and gymnastics.

The upheaval of the 1990s has had a lingering effect on sports in the region. From 1992 to 1996, Yugoslavia was banned from most international events, including World Cup soccer. At the start of the 21st century, some teams from other countries were reluctant to travel to Serbia and Montenegro out of fear of new outbreaks of violence. Today, however, this is no longer a problem.

Basketball is becoming very popular, especially among teenage boys and young men. Local teams and pickup games have popped up throughout both countries. Fans closely follow the careers of regional players who have made it to one of the European leagues or to the US National Basketball Association (NBA)—such as Serbs Nikola Jokic and newcomer Alen Smailagic.

Fencing is another popular sport in these countries. Other individual sports that have small but avid followings include gymnastics, wrestling, weight lifting, cycling, ice-skating, tennis, and track-and-field events.

At the Olympics and other international competitions, the national status of Serbia and Montengro—once part of the larger Yugoslavia, then a united federation of two states, and then two separate countries—has created challenges for athletes. For example, the seven-time Olympian shooter and 1988 gold medalist Jasna Sekaric competed under four different banners during her 24-year Olympic career. She started under the flag of Yugoslavia in 1988, then she competed as an Independent Participant in 1992, then she competed under the flag of Serbia and Montenegro from 1996 to 2004, and in 2008 and 2012 she represented Serbia.

INTERNET LINKS

http://www.bbc.com/storyworks/travel/serbia-the-place-to-be/ action-and-adventure-in-serbia
This site provides ideas for leisure-time activities in Serbia.

https://www.explore-share.com/blog/best-things-to-do -montenegro-guide-for-outdoor-lovers
Outdoor adventures in Montenegro are suggested on this travel site.

https://www.serbia.com/about-serbia/famous-serbs/sportspeople
Information about Serbian sports, athletes, and related articles can be found on this page.

FESTIVALS

A tree decorated for the holidays looks festive in the snow on a sidewalk in Belgrade.

12

WITH THEIR SHARED HISTORY, Serbia and Montenegro might be expected to have the same holidays. To some extent, that is true. The Christian feast days remain the same in both, of course, since both are majority Eastern Orthodox countries, and the most important holy days, such as Christmas and Easter, are national holidays.

During the tough times of the 1990s, the festive spirit seemed to disappear from Yugoslav life, but that spirit has enjoyed a great resurgence in the 21st century. Both religious and secular celebrations are again popular, with many festivals of both kinds taking place over the course of the year.

The main difference between the special events calendars in the two countries is seen in their national patriotic observances. Montenegro observes Independence Day on May 21 in honor of the 2006 referendum on independence, with the result of 55.5 percent of Montenegrins in favor of becoming a sovereign nation. This is different from Statehood Day, July 13, which commemorates the day in 1878 on which the Berlin Congress recognized Montenegro as an independent state.

By contrast, Serbia observes February 15 as its Statehood Day. That day marks the outbreak of the First Serbian Uprising in 1804, which eventually led to the Serbian Revolution against Ottoman rule. In turn, the revolution ultimately led to the recognition of the Serbian nation. Another layer of importance became attached to that date when, in 1835, the first modern

Since Orthodox Christmas is not traditionally a gift-giving celebration, it has no corresponding Santa figure. However, many people in Montenegro and Serbia have adopted some Western Christmas motifs, such as decorated evergreen trees and lights, for New Year's celebrations. Since the New Year is observed according to the Western calendar, December 31 and January 1 in both countries feature with great displays of fireworks.

Children play with balloons at a family festival in Belgrade's Kalemegdan Park.

Serbian constitution was adopted on that same day. Today, Serbia's official celebrations last for two days, every February 15 and 16.

Although it's not a day off from work and school, Saint Vitus's Day, or Vidovdan, on June 28 is one of Serbia's most important national and religious holidays. It commemorates the Battle of Kosovo in 1389 between the Serbs, led by Prince Lazar, and an invading army of the Ottoman Empire. Lazar died during the battle, and his forces were overcome. The Ottomans ultimately took control of the Balkan region for centuries to come. Lazar is now considered a hero, and the battle itself has become a symbol of Serb martyrdom in the face of outside aggression. It is the source of the so-called Kosovo Myth that played a critical part in the formation of Serbian national identity.

FESTIVALS FOR THE ARTS

Both countries hold a multitude of local and regional arts events. The city of Belgrade leads the parade of annual events dedicated to the arts, beginning with the annual film festival—FEST—in February. FEST draws moviemakers, critics, actors, and film buffs from all over Europe and the Middle East. By May, the city is in its full festival mode, with celebrations that includes Museum Night, when museums throughout the city open their doors for free and offer special events. The Belgrade Summer Festival begins in June and features music, dance, theater, art exhibits, and a wide variety of other special events. In September, the city hosts the Belgrade International Theatre Festival. October is a busy month in Belgrade, with the Joy of Europe International Children's Festival, as well as the separate Belgrade Children's Fair. The Balkan Cheese Festival, the Belgrade Book Fair, the Belgrade Jazz Festival, and the Belgrade Music

Festival also take place each year in October. December brings the Belgrade Winter Fun Fest.

Serbia's second-largest city, Novi Sad, also offers a series of colorful celebrations. In May, Novi Sad hosts Sterija's Theatre Festival, and in June comes the Zmaj Children's Games, a celebration of children's literature, theater, music, and poetry. In August, bands come from all over Europe for what is called the Exit Music Festival, held in the Petrovaradin Citadel. This music festival is the most famous in Serbia and one of the largest in all of Europe. This fair began as a protest against the regime of Slobodan Milosevic, but it no longer has a political intent.

Several other cities in Serbia also hold special events that attract attention beyond their local borders. One of the loudest and most popular is the Guca Trumpet Festival, also known as the Festival of Brass Bands. This riotous festival takes place in August as brass bands from all over Europe join in a noisy and joyful battle of bands.

Crowds revel in the fun at the Exit Music Festival in Novi Sad.

A DJ plays some music at the beachside Sea Dance Festival in Budva, Montenegro.

In Montenegro, there are also a number of summer music fests that attract large crowds, including the Sea Dance Festival on the beach in Budva and Bedem Fest in the city of Niksic. Special events occur year-round as well. Other well known festivals include the Mimosa Festival in the coastal town of Herceg Novi and the Kotor carnivals—the International Summer Carnival in August and the Traditional Winter Carnival in February.

EASTERN ORTHODOX HOLIDAYS

The Serbian Orthodox Church follows the Julian calendar that was established by Julius Caesar in 45 BCE. The Orthodox religious holidays therefore fall a few weeks behind those of Christian holidays on the modern (Gregorian) calendar. Therefore, Orthodox Christmas falls on January 7 and is a national holiday. Roman Catholics observing Christmas on December 25 find they are in a small minority in both Serbia and Montenegro. Similarly, Easter, which falls on a different date each spring, is also a little later in Orthodox practice. Both Orthodox Christmas and Easter are national holidays.

At Easter time in Eastern Orthodox communities, each family fills a basket with traditional Easter foods—a festive cake, dyed eggs, cheese, and butter (often in the shape of a lamb). On Easter Sunday, they take this basket to the church, where the items are placed on a long table with the goods of all the other families. The people sing as the priest walks around the table blessing all the foods.

A festive bread sits among the traditional oak leaves in a holiday arrangement for Orthodox Christmas Eve.

Christmas is celebrated on January 7. On Christmas Eve, an oak branch or log called a *badnjak* is placed on the fire as family and friends enjoy a large meal that might end with a Christmas cake containing a coin. Whoever receives the piece of cake with the coin is supposed to have good luck in the coming year. Three Sundays prior to Christmas, Detinjci (de-TEEN-tsi), or Day of the Child, is observed. The following Sunday is Mother's Day, and the third Sunday honors fathers. These three days emphasize close family ties.

PATRON SAINT'S DAY

Each Orthodox Christian family celebrates their Patron Saint's Day—Slava or Krsna Slava—a day that has been set aside to honor the family's saint or protector. The same saint is honored from generation to generation, passed down from father to son. Women take the patron saint of their husbands. This tradition's roots reach back before the arrival of Christianity, when families or tribes worshipped individual gods. Once converted to Christianity, the Serbs transferred this observance to the Christian saints.

The Slava ritual involves a series of symbols—a candle, wheat, and bread. Customs vary from region to region, but everywhere the basic idea is the same—the day is spent worshipping the patron saint by offering a bloodless sacrifice. Traditionally, the family attends church, taking with them a *slavski*

A *slavski kolac* is specially decorated for Slava.

kolac (SLAHV-skee KOH-lahk), or patron saint's cake; a bowl of cooked wheat sweetened with honey or sugar, called *koljivo* (kohl-YEE-voh); and a memorial book that lists the family's deceased relatives. The priest cuts and blesses the special cake, which is often elaborately decorated.

At home, the cake and wheat dish are placed on the table along with a candle, which is left to burn all day. Relatives and friends are invited to join in a celebration dinner. The host (always the male head of the household) prays to God and his patron saint and then serves his guests. Every guest receives a small portion of the cake and the wheat dish.

The Slava ritual is included on UNESCO's Intangible Cultural Heritage List.

THE ISLAMIC MONTH OF RAMADAN

For Muslims, the most important period is the month of Ramadan—the ninth month in Islam's calendar. The Islamic calendar is lunar, and therefore the dates do not correspond to the days of the Gregorian, or Western, calendar. As a result, the Muslim months and holidays rotate through the year. Throughout the month of Ramadan, the faithful pray and observe a strict fast every day from sunrise to sunset. Following Ramadan, the first three days in the month of Shawwal are devoted to a great festival called Eid al-Fitr, the Feast of the Fast Breaking. People gather with family and friends for three days of feasting, congregational prayers, and the exchanging of gifts. In some cities and towns, street fairs are held, featuring music and kiosks offering food for sale. Minarets are decorated with strings of little white lights.

INTERNET LINKS

https://ich.unesco.org/en/RL/slava-celebration-of-family-saint -patrons-day-01010
An explanation of Slava is provided on this UNESCO Intangible Cultural Heritage lsiting.

http://www.serbia.travel/events/events.573.html
The events calendar on this Serbia travel site is listed by month.

https://theculturetrip.com/europe/serbia/articles/the-10-best -local-festivals-in-serbia
The top music, arts, and food festivals in Serbia are introduced on this site.

https://www.timeanddate.com/holidays/montenegro
https://www.timeanddate.com/holidays/serbia
This calendar site lists the official national holidays and other special occasions in both countries.

https://www.total-montenegro-news.com/lifestyle/600-do-you -need-to-accept-an-invitation-to-slava-holiday-traditions-in -montenegro
This entry explains the patron saint celebration of Slava.

FOOD

Traditional spirals of flaky dough form *bureks*, here filled with spinach and feta cheese.

13

THE CUISINES OF SERBIA AND Montenegro reflect their geographical locations and histories. For the most part, everyday fare is similar throughout the Balkans. And given the shared history of these two particular countries, their cuisines have a great deal of overlap, with some regional variations. The foods of Montenegro and Serbia are influenced by the cuisines of Turkey, Greece, Italy, Hungary, Germany, and several other countries. No matter the country of origin, many popular recipes include meat in some form—roasts, steaks, grilled strips, ground meat, kebabs, sausages, and so on. Even breakfast usually includes meat, such as in the popular burek (BU-rek)—a pastry with layers of filling, typically cheese and ground meat.

Grilled meat is something of an obsession in Serbia and Montenegro. In fact, there's an annual festival dedicated to it in Leskovac, Serbia. Each September, the Rostiljijada (Grill Fest) attracts hungry meat lovers from all over the country, as well as abroad. The town closes its main boulevard to traffic, and the grills take over. A highlight each year is the making of the world's biggest burger, known in Serbia as *pljeskavica* (plee-ES-ka-vee-tsa).

Hungry people line up at a street grill for sizzling hot pljeskavica (beef burgers) and cevapi (sausages) on a December evening in Belgrade.

Fast foods are available everywhere, at street kiosks as well as cafés and restaurants. The most popular fast food is *cevapcici* (chay-VAP-chee-chee)—spicy sausage served on hearty pita bread. Also called *cevapi,* it's one of several foods that are often considered a national dish of Serbia.

MEALTIMES

Since most people begin work between 6 a.m. and 8 a.m., breakfast is an early, hearty meal. Tea, milk, or strong coffee is served with pastries or bread and meat or eggs, or both. For most families, the main meal of the day is served around 2 p.m. Many workers come home to eat and then resume work until 7 p.m. or 8 p.m. The meal usually begins with a thick homemade soup, followed by the main meat dish, then salad and dessert. Supper is generally a light meal and is served around 8 p.m.

REGIONAL VARIATIONS

Each region has certain specialties. In Serbia's Vojvodina province, for example, the cuisine shows a strong Hungarian influence. Many recipes call for generous portions of paprika, and Hungarian goulash comes close to being a national dish. Another spicy Vojvodina favorite is called *alaska corba* (ah-LAHS-ka CHORE-ba), which is described as a fiery river fish stew. The northern province is also known for its breads, strudels, and pastas.

Western Serbia specializes in smoked meats and lamb dishes, while the southern part of the country is renowned for its grilled meats. Zlatibor, in the mountainous western part of the country, is known for a dish that has no comparable name in the West, *komplet lepinja*, which is said to be "a flat

A meaty goulash with mashed potatoes is a hearty meal inspired by Hungarian cuisine.

PAPRIKA

Outdoor markets throughout Serbia and Montenegro sell many varieties of paprika. Paprika seasoning ranges from mild to very hot. The fruit of the Capsicum annuum *plant is sold fresh or dried, and eaten raw, cooked, pickled, or ground into paprika powder. Each of these forms is featured in former Yugoslav cuisine.*

Red peppers dry on the side of a house in Donja Lokosnica, Serbia.

Paprika often flavors a filling of rice and meat or cheese used in stuffed vegetables such as bell peppers. A bit of yogurt or sour cream may be served to take away the heat of the paprika.

In general, hot and spicy foods are common in both Serbia and Montenegro. Spices such as paprika and peppers are often used to give foods added flavor and heat. Dried peppers can be used to spice up many Serbian and Montenegrin dishes.

bun with everything in it." Actually, it's a round bread hollowed out and filled with cream and egg, baked—ideally in a wood-fired stove—and then a brown, salty condiment called *pretop* is spread on it. The pretop is derived from the fat and juices of a lamb or pork roast.

Montenegrin cuisine also varies geographically. The food of the northern highland region differs somewhat from that of the coastal area. Coastal cuisine is traditionally more Mediterranean and Italian in style, with seafood being a common dish. Olive oil, lemon, parsley, bay leaves, and garlic are common seasonings. Inland, the Montenegrin menu becomes heartier and more similar to Serbian fare. Meals are more often based on beef or lamb, potatoes, cheese, bread, and rich dairy products.

SERBIAN DISHES

The foods of Serbia are famous in their own right, especially the grilled meat, including cevapcici and pljeskavica—something like a large hamburger, but very spicy. (This, too, is a popular fast food.) Another well-known grilled dish is the Serbian version of shish kebab, called *raznjici* (razh-NYEE-chee)—made with chunks of veal or pork on a skewer with onions and peppers. Another typical Serbian dish is *duvec* (JEW-vech)—grilled pork cutlets mixed with spiced stewed peppers, zucchini, and tomatoes and served over rice. Just about all of these foods are heavily spiced. Even Serbian salad is anything but subtle. It often features raw peppers with sliced onions and tomatoes and a dressing of oil and vinegar.

A pljeskavica is served with pita bread, cheese, and a roasted red pepper condiment.

Serbia is a land of ravishing red raspberries. The taste and aroma of Serbian raspberries are said to be uniquely luscious, due to the country's rich soil and climatic conditions. Raspberries are grown on small family farms throughout most of Serbia, but the greatest concentration of raspberry growers is in Arilje, in the western part of the country. Each year, Arilje hosts a Raspberry Days celebration.

Rows of raspberries grow on a mountain farm.

For years, Serbia was one of the world's top raspberry producers. In fact, in 2015, it was the top raspberry grower in the world. Although its standing in world production has slipped in recent years, the country is still known for the exceptional quality of its "red gold." In 2018, Serbia produced around 140,000 tons (127,000 metric tons) of raspberries, but adverse weather caused a loss of 80 percent of the following year's crop.

Serbia exports its raspberries in frozen form, but locals can enjoy the fresh bounty. Serbs make a thin fruit preserve called slatko, *which can be made with a wide variety of fruits, but raspberry slatko is a favorite. It's usually enjoyed by itself, served in small amounts in little bowls with a spoon. Serbs also make raspberry jam, pies, fruit salads, and ice cream.*

MONTENEGRIN DISHES

Regional recipes from Montenegro often include dairy products. These foods include a favorite called *kajmak* (KAJ-mak), made with cream, which is then salted and allowed to harden. The Greek influence is evident in *musaka* (MU-sa-ka)— eggplant and potatoes placed in alternating layers with ground meat (either lamb or beef). Recipes with a Turkish or Middle Eastern touch include shish kebab and *kapama* (kah-PAH-mah)—stewed lamb mixed with spinach, onions, and yogurt. The Middle Eastern influence is also found in dishes such as *sarma* (SAR-ma), or stuffed cabbage rolls, and *punjene tikvice* (PUN-je-na TEEK-vee-tsa), or stuffed zucchini. In both dishes, the filling is ground beef or lamb and rice.

FRUIT AND DESSERTS

In most families, desserts are light—a simple cake or pudding and whatever fruits are available, with plums being an unofficial national fruit. Apples, grapes, melons, pomegranates, and pears are also popular. On special occasions, a family will have baklava, an import from Turkey, or Viennese-style tortes.

The fruits of Serbia and Montenegro are also used to make wines and brandies. Serbian and Montenegrin wines are highly regarded and are sold worldwide. In Serbia, the most popular alcoholic drink is a plum brandy called *sljivovica* (SHLYEE-vo-vee-tsa), but Montenegrins prefer a potent grape brandy.

INTERNET LINKS

https://meanderbug.com/montenegro-traditional-food
This travel site provides an overview of Montenegrin cuisine, with photos.

http://www.serbia.com/about-serbia/traditional-cuisine
This site offers several articles about Serbian cuisine.

https://theculturetrip.com/europe/serbia/articles/11-traditional -serbian-dishes-you-need-to-try
Popular Serbian dishes are shown in photos on this site.

CEVAPI (GRILLED SAUSAGES)

Also called *cevapcici*, these sausages are popular in both Serbia and Montenegro and throughout the Balkan region.

¾ pound (350 grams) ground beef
¾ pound (350 g) ground lamb or pork
3 tablespoons finely grated onion
1 tablespoon freshly minced garlic
1 ½ teaspoons paprika
1 ½ teaspoons kosher salt
1 ½ teaspoons freshly ground black pepper
¾ teaspoon baking soda

In a medium bowl, mix together beef, lamb or pork, onion, garlic, paprika, salt, pepper, and baking soda by hand until thoroughly combined.

Form meat mixture into finger-length sausages (about 3 inches long by ¾ inch wide, or 7.5 centimeters by 2 centimeters).

Ask an adult to help grill the sausages. Heat a grill to medium-high heat. Oil the grilling grate. Grill sausages over medium-high direct heat until well browned on all sides and just cooked through, about 8 minutes total. Remove to a serving tray or plates, and let rest for 5 minutes.

Serve with sliced sweet onions, *kajmak* (a creamy dairy product; to approximate, mix ½ cup crumbled feta cheese, 1 cup sour cream, and ½ pound softened cream cheese until smooth), *ajvar* (roasted red pepper spread), and flatbread, such as pita.

VANILICE (LITTLE VANILLA COOKIES)

These dainty Serbian cookies are served on holidays and special occasions.

1 cup (250 grams) butter
½ cup (125 g) sugar
4 ½ cups (500 g) flour
½ teaspoon vanilla extract
1 egg and 1 egg yolk
1 teaspoon lemon zest, finely grated
pinch of salt
apricot jam
plain or vanilla confectioner's (powdered) sugar

In a mixer fitted with the paddle attachment, beat the butter and sugar until light and creamy. Add the egg, egg yolk, lemon zest, vanilla, and salt, and beat well until combined. Add the flour, a little at a time, and mix just until combined.

Using hands, shape dough into a ball. Flatten into a disc, wrap in plastic, and refrigerate for at least 1 hour.

Preheat the oven to 350°F (175°C).

Roll the dough out to about ¼ inch (or ½ cm) thick, and cut out circles with a small round cookie cutter, about 1 ½ inches (4 cm) wide. Reroll and cut out more cookies until dough is all cut. Place on a baking sheet lined with parchment paper, about 1 inch (2.5 cm) apart. Bake for 12 minutes until firm. The cookies should still be quite pale. Remove from the oven and let sit 5 minutes on the baking sheet; then transfer to a wire rack to cool.

Spread jam on the flat side of half the cookies and top with the rest of the cookies, flat sides down, to make a sandwich. Don't use too much jam on each cookie; it should not squeeze out the sides. Sprinkle cookies with confectioner's sugar. Place them in an airtight tin before serving.

Adriatic Sea, A4, A5, B5

Albania, B4—B5

Balkan Mountains, D3—D4

Bar, A5

Belgrade, B2

Beocin, B2

Black Lake, A4

Bor, D3

Bosnia-Herzegovina, A2—A4, B2—B3

Budva, A5

Budva Bay, A5

Bulgaria, D3—D5

Cacak, B3

Cetinje, A5

Croatia, A1—A2, B2, A4—A5

Danube (river), A1, A2, B2, C2, D2, D3

Dinaric Alps, A4

Djerdap, D2

Drava (river), A1

Gracanica, C4

Guca, B3

Gulf of Kotor, A5

Herceg Novi, A5

Hungary, A1—B1

Ibar (river), B3—B4

Iron Gate, D2

Kopaonik, B4

Kopaonik Mountains, B4, C4

Kotor, A5

Kosovo , B4, B5, C4, C5

Kragujevac, C3

Kraljevo, B3

Lake Skadar, A5, B5

Mededi Potok, C4

Mount Avala, B2

Mount Deravica, B4—B5

Mount Durmitor, A4

Niksic, A4

Nis, C4

North Macedonia, B5, C5, D5

Novi Sad, B2

Novi Sip, D2

Pannonian Plain, A1, B1—B2, C2

Pec, B4

Petrovaradin, B2

Podgorica, A5

Pozarevac, C2

Presevo, C5

Pristina, C4

Prizren, B5

Rekovac, C3

Romania, C1, C2, D1—D3

Sava (river), B2

Sharr Mountains, B5, C5

Smederevo, C2

Sokobanja, C3

Sremska Mitrovica, B2

Stari Bar, A5

Subotica, B1

Sveti Stefan, A5

Tara (river), A4, B4

Tisa (river), B1—B2

Vitina, C5

Vojvodina, A1—A2, B1—B2, C2

Zabljak, A4

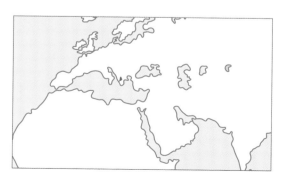

ECONOMIC SERBIA AND MONTENEGRO

Services

Airport

Port

Tourism

Natural Resources

Coal

CP Copper

Hydroelectricity

Natural Gas

Oil

Timber

Manufacturing

AI Aluminum

Cement

Electrical Appliances

Oil Refinery

Processed Foods

Textiles

Vehicles

SERBIA

MONTENEGRO

KOSOVO

Agriculture

Cattle

Fruit

Pigs

Plums

Potatoes

Sheep

Soybeans

Sugar Beets

Sunflower Seeds

Wheat

ABOUT THE ECONOMY

All statistics are 2017 estimates unless otherwise noted.

SERBIA

GDP (OFFICIAL EXCHANGE RATE)
$41.43 billion

GDP PER CAPITA
$15,100

LABOR FORCE
2.92 million

LABOR FORCE BY OCCUPATION
agriculture: 19.4 percent
industry: 24.5 percent
services: 56.1 percent

UNEMPLOYMENT RATE
14.1 percent

CURRENCY
Serbian dinar (RSD)
$1 US dollar = 106.66 Serbian dinars (2019)

AGRICULTURAL PRODUCTS
wheat, maize, sunflower seeds, sugar
beets, fruits, vegetables, beef, pork, other
meat products, dairy products, wine

INDUSTRIES
automobiles, base metals, furniture, food
processing, machinery, chemicals, sugar,
tires, clothes, pharmaceuticals

MONTENEGRO

GDP (OFFICIAL EXCHANGE RATE)
$4.784 billion

GDP PER CAPITA
$17,800

LABOR FORCE
273,200

LABOR FORCE BY OCCUPATION
agriculture: 7.9 percent
industry: 17.1 percent
services: 75 percent

UNEMPLOYMENT RATE
16.1 percent

CURRENCY
Euro
$1 US dollar = 0.91 euro (2019)

AGRICULTURAL PRODUCTS
tobacco, potatoes, citrus fruits, olives and
related products, grapes, sheep, wine

INDUSTRIES
steelmaking, aluminum, agricultural
processing, consumer goods, tourism

CULTURAL SERBIA AND MONTENEGRO

Gallery of Frescoes
Housed in the National Museum, the gallery houses reproductions of the famous frescoes found in churches and monasteries throughout the former Yugoslavia.

Kalemegdan Citadel
Built in the fourth century CE, the Belgrade Fortress is one of the Serbia's most famous landmarks.

Skadarska Street
This restored area of Old Town Belgrade has shops, cafés, and cobblestone streets.

Petrovaradin Fortress
Built in the 1700s, the citadel is on the banks of the Danube River in Novi Sad.

National Theatre
Built in 1868, the theater houses ballet, opera, and drama ensembles.

Sremska Mitrovica
This city is built on the ruins of the ancient Roman city of Sirmium, birthplace of five Roman emperors.

SERBIA

Danube River
The famous Iron Gates gorge squeezes the Danube River through a dramatic canyon.

Durmitor National Park
This beautiful resort area with 18 mountain lakes is popular for hiking, swimming, fishing, and other outdoor activities.

Tara Canyon
This canyon is second only to the Grand Canyon for its depth and length.

MONTENEGRO

KOSOVO

Kalenic Monastery
Located near Rekovac in Serbia, it is an early 15th century Orthodox monastery.

Zabljak
This picturesque ski resort is the highest town in Montenegro.

Lake Skadar
Montenegro's largest lake, on the border with Albania, is a popular tourist attraction known for excellent fishing.

Kosovo Plain
Site of the historic 14th-century battle in which the Ottoman Turks defeated the Serbian army. The battle is the subject of many folktales, songs, and poems.

ABOUT THE CULTURE

All statistics are 2011 estimates unless otherwise stated. Note: In Serbia, most ethnic Albanians boycotted the 2011 census, which impacts the figures given here.

OFFICIAL NAME
Republic of Serbia

CAPITAL
Belgrade

POPULATION
7,078,110 (2018)

POPULATION GROWTH RATE
—0.47 percent (2018)

ETHNIC GROUPS
Serb 83.3 percent, Hungarian 3.5 percent, Roma 2.1 percent, Bosniak 2 percent, other 5.7 percent

RELIGIONS
Orthodox 84.6 percent, Catholic 5 percent, Muslim 3.1 percent, Protestant 1 percent, atheist 1.1 percent, other 0.8 percent

LANGUAGES
Serbian (official) 88.1 percent, Hungarian 3.4 percent, Bosnian 1.9 percent, Romani 1.4 percent, other 3.4 percent

OFFICIAL NAME
Montenegro

CAPITAL
Podgorica; Cetinje retains the status of "Old Royal Capital"

POPULATION
614,249 (2018)

POPULATION GROWTH RATE
—0.34 percent (2018)

ETHNIC GROUPS
Montenegrin 45 percent, Serbian 28.7 percent, Bosniak 8.7 percent, Albanian 4.9 percent, Muslim 3.3 percent, Roma 1 percent, Croatian 1 percent, other 2.6 percent

RELIGIONS
Orthodox 72.1 percent, Muslim 19.1 percent, Catholic 3.4 percent, atheist 1.2 percent, other 1.5 percent

LANGUAGES
Serbian 42.9 percent, Montenegrin (official) 37 percent, Bosnian 5.3 percent, Albanian 5.3 percent, Serbo-Croatian 2 percent, other 3.5 percent

TIMELINE

IN SERBIA AND MONTENEGRO	IN THE WORLD
228 BCE Romans establish the Province of Illyricum.	
300s CE Barbarian groups invade the Balkans.	
600 Slavic tribes migrate into Balkans. South Slavs dominate the area of future Yugoslavia.	**600** The Maya civilization reaches its height.
700–900 The entire region becomes part of the Byzantine Empire; Saints Cyril and Methodius spread Orthodox Christianity.	**1000** The Chinese perfect gunpowder and begin to use it in warfare.
1389 Ottoman Turks defeat the Serbs in the Battle of Kosovo.	**1530** The transatlantic slave trade begins, organized by the Portuguese in Africa.
	1776 The US Declaration of Independence is signed.
1804–1815 Serbs rise up against Turkish rule.	
1830 The independence of Serbia is recognized by the great powers of Europe.	**1861–1865** The American Civil War is fought.
1912–1913 The Balkan Wars are fought.	**1914** World War I begins.
1918 The Kingdom of Serbs, Croats, and Slovenes is established.	**1923** The Soviet Union is established following Russian Revolution.
1929 The kingdom's name is changed to Yugoslavia.	
1934 Croatian terrorists assassinate King Alexander.	**1939** World War II begins.
1941 Germany invades Yugoslavia.	
1945 Marshal Tito becomes head of Yugoslavia; he establishes a communist government.	**1969** US astronaut Neil Armstrong becomes the first human on the moon.

IN SERBIA AND MONTENEGRO	IN THE WORLD
1980 Tito dies.	
	1986 A nuclear power disaster rocks Chernobyl, Ukraine.
1991–1992 Croatia, Slovenia, and Bosnia-Herzegovina declare independence from Yugoslavia.	**1991** The Soviet Union breaks up.
1995 The Srebrenica Massacre occurs; NATO air strikes force Serbs to sign the Dayton Accords.	**1997** Britain returns Hong Kong to China.
2000–2001 Slobodan Milosevic is arrested and extradited to the Netherlands for trial.	**2001** Al-Qaeda terrorists stage 9/11 attacks in the United States.
2003 Yugoslavia becomes the Union of Serbia and Montenegro. Serbian prime minister Zoran Djindjic is assassinated in Belgrade.	**2003** The Iraq War begins.
2006 Milosevic is found dead in his cell in The Hague. Montenegro declares independence.	
2008 Kosovo declares independence.	**2008** The United States elects its first African American president, Barack Obama.
2010 Serbia and Kosovo sign an agreement normalizing relations.	
2014 Serbia's EU membership talks begin.	
2015 Serbia makes its first arrests of people accused of the 1995 Srebrenica Massacre.	**2015–2016** ISIS launches terror attacks in Belgium and France.
2017 Montenegro joins NATO.	**2017** Donald Trump becomes US president.
2019 Montenegro passses controversial law in opposition to Serbian Orthodox Church.	**2019** Notre Dame Cathedral in Paris is damaged by fire. Donald Trump is impeached.
2020 Serbia and Kosovo agree to resume passenger and cargo flights between their capitals for the first time in more than two decades.	**2020** Deadly coronavirus epidemic spreads around the world.

GLOSSARY

Balkans
The countries occupying the Balkan Peninsula.

bora
An icy wind that sweeps down from the north, bringing little snow but bitter cold.

Bosniaks
Bosnians who are Muslims.

cevapcici (ce-VAP-chee-chee)
A popular Yugoslav fast food—a sausage stuffed with ground meat and spices.

Eid al-Fitr
The Feast of the Fast Breaking, which ends the Muslim holy month of Ramadan.

ethnic cleansing
A process in which one ethnic group expels, imprisons, or kills civilians of another ethnic group, usually a minority.

extradite
To hand over a person (usually one accused of a crime) to a foreign country to be tried in court.

fresco
A painting done in water-based pigments on wet plaster, usually on a wall or ceiling, so the colors penetrate the plaster and become fixed as the plaster dries.

gajde (GEI-de)
A musical instrument that looks like a set of bagpipes.

Iron Gate
A famous narrow channel walled by high cliffs in the Danube River.

karst terrain
Areas of limestone where water has eroded softer limestone, creating depressions and many caves.

kumstvo (KUM-stvo)
A form of family patronage.

Partisans
Yugoslav freedom fighters against Germany in World War II, led by Marshal Tito.

seminomadic
Refrerring to a lifestyle in which people move to temporary dwellings during certain seasons or as they look for food.

zupan (ZOO-pahn)
A Serb clan leader.

FOR FURTHER INFORMATION

BOOKS

Armatta, Judith. *Twilight of Impunity: The War Crimes Trial of Slobodan Milosevic*. Durham, NC: Duke University Press Books, 2010.

DK Eyewitness. *Serbia*. New York, NY: Dorling Kindersley Publishing, 2016.

Sheward, Tamara, and Peter Dragicevich. *Montenegro*. Lonely Planet Travel Guide. Melbourne, Australia: Lonely Planet Global, Inc., 2017.

Zmukic, Lara. *Serbia: Culture Smart! The Essential Guide to Customs & Culture*. London, UK: Kuperard, 2012.

ONLINE

Balkan Insight. https://balkaninsight.com.

BBC News. "Montenegro Country Profile." https://www.bbc.com/news/world-europe-17667132.

BBC News. "Serbia Country Profile." https://www.bbc.com/news/world-europe-17907947.

CIA. *The World Factbook*. "Montenegro." https://www.cia.gov/library/publications/the-world-factbook/geos/mj.html.

CIA. *The World Factbook*. "Serbia." https://www.cia.gov/library/publications/the-world-factbook/geos/ri.html.

Discover Montenegro. https://www.discover-montenegro.com/en.

Encyclopedia Britannica. "Montenegro." https://www.britannica.com/place/Montenegro.

Encyclopedia Britannica. "Serbia." https://www.britannica.com/place/Serbia.

National Tourism Organization of Serbia. http://www.serbia.travel/home.779.html.

MUSIC

Folk Dance Ensemble Vila. *Music of Serbia*. ARC Music, 2008.

Serbian Choral Society "Jedinstvo" 1839 Kotor. *Orthodox Church Music from Montenegro*. Soliton, 2016.

Serbia: Traditional Music. ARC Music, 2011.

VIDEO

Brasslands. Meerkat Media, 2014.

BIBLIOGRAPHY

BBC News. "Montenegro Country Profile." https://www.bbc.com/news/world-europe-17667132.

BBC News. "Serbia Country Profile." https://www.bbc.com/news/world-europe-17907947.

CIA. *The World Factbook*. "Kosovo." https://www.cia.gov/library/publications/the-world-factbook/geos/kv.html.

CIA. *The World Factbook*. "Montenegro." https://www.cia.gov/library/publications/the-world-factbook/geos/mj.html.

CIA. *The World Factbook*. "Serbia." https://www.cia.gov/library/publications/the-world-factbook/geos/ri.html.

Discover Montenegro. https://www.discover-montenegro.com/en.

Encyclopedia Britannica. "Montenegro." https://www.britannica.com/place/Montenegro.

Encyclopedia Britannica. "Serbia." https://www.britannica.com/place/Serbia.

Garsevic, Srdjan. "Almost Forgotten, Serbian National Museum Reopens." *Balkan Insight*, June 29, 2018. https://balkaninsight.com/2018/06/29/almost-forgotten-serbian-national-museum-reopens-06-28-2018.

Glusac, Elaine. "Returning to Montenegro." *New York Times*, August 22, 2018. https://www.nytimes.com/2018/08/22/travel/montenegro.html.

Hewitt, Simon. "Serbia Recovers From 'Cultural Genocide.'" *Art Newspaper*, June 20, 2018. https://www.theartnewspaper.com/news/serbia-recovers-from-cultural-genocide.

Hix, Lisa. "A Frenzy of Trumpets: Why Brass Musicians Can't Resist Serbia's Wildest Festival." *Collectors Weekly*, November 15, 2013. https://www.collectorsweekly.com/articles/why-brass-musicians-cant-resist-serbias-wildest-festival.

Lonely Planet. "Montenegro." https://www.lonelyplanet.com/montenegro.

Lonely Planet. "Serbia." https://www.lonelyplanet.com/serbia.

Simons, Marlise, and Alison Smale. "Slobodan Milosevic, 64, Former Yugoslav Leader Accused of War Crimes, Dies." *New York Times*, March 12, 2006. https://www.nytimes.com/2006/03/12/world/europe/slobodan-milosevic-64-former-yugoslav-leader-accused-of-war.html.

UNESCO World Heritage Convention. "Montenegro." https://whc.unesco.org/en/statesparties/me.

UNESCO World Heritage Convention. "Serbia." https://whc.unesco.org/en/statesparties/rs.

INDEX

INDEX